AFFORDABLE COURSE MATERIALS

AN ALCTS MONOGRAPH

AFFORDABLE COURSE MATERIALS

Electronic Textbooks and Open Educational Resources

EDITED BY CHRIS DIAZ

An imprint of the American Library Association

CHICAGO 2017

CHRIS DIAZ is the digital publishing services librarian at Northwestern University (Evanston, Illinois), where he manages the institutional repository and the library's digital publishing program. He became interested in college textbooks and open educational resources when he was the collections management librarian at National Louis University (Chicago).

© 2017 by the American Library Association

Extensive effort has gone into ensuring the reliability of the information in this book; however, the publisher makes no warranty, express or implied, with respect to the material contained herein.

ISBNS
978-0-8389-1580-6 (paper)
978-0-8389-1594-3 (PDF)
978-0-8389-1595-0 (ePub)
978-0-8389-1596-7 (Kindle)

Library of Congress Cataloging-in-Publication Data

Names: Diaz, Chris, 1988- editor.
Title: Affordable course materials : electronic textbooks and open educational resources / edited by Chris Diaz.
Description: Chicago : ALA Editions, an imprint of the American Library Association, 2017. | Series: An ALCTS monograph | Includes bibliographical references and index.
Identifiers: LCCN 2017012318| ISBN 9780838915806 (pbk. : alk. paper) | ISBN 9780838915943 (pdf) | ISBN 9780838915950 (epub) | ISBN 9780838915967 (Kindle)
Subjects: LCSH: Academic libraries—Collection development. | Libraries—Special collections—Electronic textbooks. | Open access publishing. | College textbooks—Prices—United States. | Libraries and colleges—United States—Case studies. | Academic libraries—United States—Case studies.
Classification: LCC Z675.U5 A4147 2017 | DDC 025.2/1877—dc23 LC record available at https://lccn.loc.gov/2017012318

Cover image © Sergey Nivens, Adobe Stock.

Text composition by Dianne M. Rooney in the Adobe Caslon Pro and Archer typefaces.

♾ This paper meets the requirements of ANSI/NISO Z39.48–1992 (Permanence of Paper).

Printed in the United States of America

21 20   19   18   17   5   4   3   2   1

CONTENTS

INTRODUCTION

Collecting the Curriculum

"What if I just bought all the textbooks?" This is the question I asked myself in the summer of 2015, one year into my job as the collections librarian of a small, private, broad-access university.[1] At the time, I had difficulty planning a collections strategy for the 2015–16 academic year because our monographic acquisitions budget had been cut by 30 percent and our faculty were being encouraged to redesign or develop courses in an online or blended instructional model, thereby reducing the amount of time students and faculty would spend on campus.[2] I needed to make a small amount of money have a meaningful impact, so textbooks seemed like the obvious place to start.

However, with a collection spread across four library locations at a university with six campuses moving toward more online and blended academic programming, print textbook reserves were out of the question. E-books were already a preferred book format for us, so I decided to investigate the availability of textbooks in the e-book format.

I started with the campus bookstore. National Louis University does not have a brick-and-mortar bookstore but uses an online vendor, a relationship managed by the Student Services Department. The bookstore liaison sent me a spreadsheet containing course title, instructor, book title, publisher, and ISBN information for textbooks assigned in the upcoming quarter. This spreadsheet contained about 600 rows, so I de-duplicated the ISBN column down to 394 ISBNs.

With the ISBNs, I ran a search in our vendor catalog and found that roughly 25 percent of the textbooks were available electronically under a multiuser license.[3] The prices for the licenses ranged from $13.99 to $243.00, with an average of $113.17 per multiuser perpetual access license. The total cost for the books was about 17 percent of our annual book budget.[4] Our book budget is used to support the education, business, human services, and social sciences curricular areas with a preference for e-books. As a teaching and practitioner-focused university with access to over eighty academic library collections in Illinois, it was not our mission to collect the scholarly record.[5] These electronic textbooks therefore fit our collecting scope, and they were essentially guaranteed to be used. I ordered the e-books immediately.

This was the easy part. It was not enough to buy e-books and catalog them; people needed to know that they are available. Providing electronic access to nearly 1 in 5 required textbooks for a university merits announcement. Using the original spreadsheet information, I matched each textbook with the course that had assigned it. Using the course catalog and university website, I recorded the name and e-mail address of either the instructor or program chair. I sent tailored e-mails to instructors and program chairs with the catalog record URLs of the e-books and suggested they add these links to their syllabi or online courses.[6] I also copied the deans of the colleges.[7]

E-mailing instructors and program chairs the catalog links was by far the most time-consuming—and time-sensitive—part of the project. I sent tailored e-mails that included the following information:

- I introduced myself as the librarian responsible for developing library collections in support of their teaching and research.
- I included a brief overview of how textbook prices can affect student success.[8]
- I provided a list of the textbooks they were using with links to the e-book versions in the catalog, noting any relevant licensing limitations of the e-books.
- I offered assistance with using e-books in courses and selecting open or library-licensed textbooks for any future curriculum development or redesign.

As both a collections librarian and an advocate for open educational resources (OER), I found this to be a very effective method to market library resources and make connections on campus for OER advocacy.[9]

Of course, using the e-book versions of textbooks can be as problematic as any other library-licensed e-book, and this fact needs to be communicated with every promise to provide electronic access to course readings. In all of my e-mails and conversations to faculty and administrators about this e-book/textbook project, I made sure to explain that the e-books are textbook alternatives;

they are not replacements. The students who have the means to purchase the print versions of textbooks should be encouraged to do so, but for everyone else, this is another option.

The response rate to this e-mail campaign was fairly high. Most instructors responded with a thank-you, several had questions about how e-books work, and a few asked me to check on the e-book availability of the other books they were using or planning to use. In the months that followed, I became associated with the issues of textbook affordability and OER. I gave presentations at college, department, and faculty senate meetings about textbook affordability, OER, and library e-books. In one extreme case, an associate dean instituted a policy whereby courses within his portfolio needed to either assign open textbooks, library e-books, journal articles from library-licensed databases, or no textbooks at all. Academic freedom notwithstanding, this was a boon for library e-book collections and OER advocacy.

There is another story here. Higher education is under intense budgetary scrutiny. This scrutiny has introduced a "data-driven" mindset to administration and planning, both within and beyond academic libraries. To demonstrate the value of library collections, I began thinking about the buying power libraries provide their campuses and the ways in which that buying power can save students money. I wanted to illustrate this through the use of these e-books.

Library-provided access to electronic textbooks increases accessibility for students in online classes and students who work full-time. The books are available twenty-four hours a day, seven days a week, and many of the e-book platforms include search, citation, and screen-reading features. Conservatively speaking, let us assume that there is one required textbook per course. If a student takes five courses with the average cost of each print textbook estimated at $58.67, the student is looking at a textbook bill of $293.35 for the semester. If one of every five textbooks is available electronically through the library, the e-books could save one student $117.34 over an academic year, reducing that student's textbook costs by 20 percent. For the price of one multiuser license, the impact of this single-use case can be replicated by the number of students for whom the e-book is required and rolls over each subsequent semester the e-book is assigned. The savings for students are significant, and the library supports the institution with affordable course materials that potentially help reduce the overall cost of attendance and increase student retention.

Despite the relative success of this project, I felt like a bad librarian. Using course reading lists as a basis for collection development felt like cheating, as if I were abdicating my responsibility as a subject specialist to develop a strong and useful collection by other means. I took this question to an Association for Library Collections and Technical Services discussion group at the American Library Association's Midwinter Meeting in Boston in 2016. There, I learned that librarians at large and small, public and private, and selective and nonselective colleges and universities are approaching course materials, electronic textbooks, and OER in a number of interesting and innovative ways.

This edited volume of case studies discusses how academic libraries are responding to the demand for college textbooks by acquiring or encouraging the use of affordable course materials. These library-led, affordable textbook initiatives include marketing and managing institutional grant programs for faculty to replace commercial textbooks with library collections and OER; working with college bookstores to share course adoption lists and developing efficient workflows for e-book acquisition; creating an online database for faculty to discover, request, and adopt electronic textbooks; supporting an international branch campus with 100 percent textbook and course materials coverage provided by the library; partnering with instructional designers to integrate affordable course materials into the curriculum; and analyzing humanities and social sciences syllabi for OER and library outreach opportunities.

Electronic textbooks and advocating for OER present new ways that librarians can promote library collections and lend their expertise toward creating a more equitable learning experience for college students. As this book discusses, both e-book technology and OER are designed to support immediate online access to large groups of users all over the world, yet both produce their own set of challenges for librarians. The biggest challenge in taking an advocacy stance on textbook affordability may be convincing faculty to rethink the textbooks they assign and to undertake the work involved in moving the curriculum away from expensive textbooks when free or more affordable options are already available. Overcoming this challenge requires respecting academic freedom, while also ensuring that faculty are aware of the quality OER available and their efficacy on student learning outcomes.[10] The case studies in this book are a guide for academic librarians interested in textbook affordability and in offering solutions that may be implemented at both large and small institutions.

Notes

1. Davis Jenkins and Olga Rodriguez, "Access and Success with Less: Improving Productivity in Broad-Access Postsecondary Institutions," *Future of Children* 23 (Spring 2013): 188, http://futureofchildren.org/publications/docs/23_01_09.pdf. Jenkins and

Rodriguez define broad-access as "community colleges and less-selective public four-year colleges and universities" that "have completion rates lower than those of selective institutions and are struggling financially." Although it is private and nonprofit, this definition fits National Louis University during the time when I was employed there.

2. Educause, "Blended Learning" (2017), https://library.educause.edu/topics/teaching -and-learning/blended-learning. Blended or "hybrid" learning combines online and face-to-face elements in course instruction. At National Louis University, students in a blended course would meet face-to-face once per month, and online once or several times per week for the duration of the course.

3. When I say "multiuser" license, I mean either three-user, loan-limited concurrent licenses (such as ProQuest's "non-linear" or EBSCO's "concurrent" options) or unlimited user licenses.

4. The average price for the print version was $58.67.

5. National Louis University is an I-share member of the Consortium for Academic and Research Libraries in Illinois (CARLI), https://www.carli.illinois.edu/membership/ i-share_part.

6. National Louis University uses Desire2Learn's (D2L) Learning Management System for all of its courses.

7. I recommend using discretion here. I had a good working relationship with many of the college deans and university administrators at the time, and I knew that the textbook cost issue was of great interest to them because of its impact on cost of attendance and student retention.

8. Ethan Senack, "Fixing the Broken Textbook Market: How Students Respond to High Textbook Costs and Demand Alternatives," Student PIRGs, www.studentpirgs .org/reports/sp/fixing-broken-textbook-market. I specifically referenced the rate at which students decide against purchasing a textbook because of the cost, which is 65 percent.

9. Open educational resources (OER) are learning objects that are available online free of charge and that are free of most copyright and licensing restrictions. While OER can include a number of types of learning objects, this book focuses on textbooks. For a more thorough discussion on OER, see David Wiley, T. J. Bliss, and Mary McEwen, "Open Educational Resources: A Review of the Literature," in *Handbook of Research on Educational Communications and Technology,* ed. J. Michael Spector, M. David Merrill, Jan Elen, and M. J. Bishop (New York: Springer, 2014), doi: 10.1007/978–1 -4614–3185–5_63.

10. John Hilton III, "Open Educational Resources and College Textbook Choices: A Review of Research on Efficacy and Perceptions," *Education Technology Research and Development* 64, no. 4 (2016): 573, doi: 10.1007/s11423–016–9434–9. This review of

research shows that OER generally produces the same learning outcomes as commercial textbooks at a significantly lower cost to the student.

Bibliography

Educause. "Blended Learning" (2017). Educause | Library. https://library.educause.edu/topics/teaching-and-learning/blended-learning.

Hilton, John, III. "Open Educational Resources and College Textbook Choices: A Review of Research on Efficacy and Perceptions." *Education Technology Research and Development* 64, no. 4 (2016): 573–90. doi: 10.1007/s11423–016–9434–9.

Jenkins, Davis, and Olga Rodriguez. "Access and Success with Less: Improving Productivity in Broad-Access Postsecondary Institutions." *Future of Children* 23, no. 1 (2013): 188. http://futureofchildren.org/futureofchildren/publications/journals/article/index.xml?journalid=79&articleid=586.

Senack, Ethan. "Fixing the Broken Textbook Market: How Students Respond to High Textbook Costs and Demand Alternatives." Student PIRGs. www.studentpirgs.org/reports/sp/fixing-broken-textbook-market.

Wiley, David, T. J. Bliss, and Mary McEwen. "Open Educational Resources: A Review of the Literature." In *Handbook of Research on Educational Communications and Technology,* ed. J. Michael Spector, M. David Merrill, Jan Elen, and M. J. Bishop. New York: Springer, 2014. doi: 10.1007/978–1–4614–3185–5_63.

ONE SIZE FITS NONE
The UCLA Library's Customized Approach to Course Materials

Sharon E. Farb and Dawn Setzler

I t began in the summer of 2012 with what seemed like a simple question: "What's a textbook?"

The question arose amid increasing public attention paid to the cost of course materials in higher education. These high prices were clearly of concern to students and their parents, and in response, the open educational resources movement was gaining momentum. The U.S. Congress introduced legislation to address this problem, and in fall 2012 California passed two laws aimed at creating a library of free and lower-cost instructional materials for use in the state's public community colleges and universities.

At UCLA, the scale of the need to keep course materials affordable was evident. More than a third of its undergraduate students are Pell Grant recipients; more than half receive some federal, state, or campus financial aid; and nearly half graduate with loans they, not their parents, are obligated to pay back.[1] UCLA's undergraduate admissions website estimated that course materials totaled $1,599 per student for the 2012–13 academic year, an effective 12 percent addition to basic tuition and fees.[2]

The California Master Plan for Higher Education enshrined the ideal of a public higher education system that combined exceptional quality with broad accessibility and affordability.[3] It produced the state's comprehensive network of community colleges, four-year colleges, and research universities. The master plan's ideals continue to inspire the University of California's mission, and its goals remain a guiding philosophy on each campus, including at UCLA.

Mindful of all of this context, library administrators and scholarly communication staff began to consider the textbook question. Related questions flew thick and fast. How many courses at UCLA use traditional textbooks? How are those books chosen? How many UCLA faculty members are textbook authors, and are their books being used in UCLA courses? Is anyone else at UCLA doing anything to lower textbook costs? Why should efforts to lower textbook prices be based in a university library? What are other academic libraries doing?

The last question was the first to be answered: the libraries at the University of Massachusetts, Amherst, and Temple University had launched noteworthy programs.[4] Locally, the UCLA Store had taken steps to lower textbook prices, and the undergraduate student government had funded both a textbook lending library and textbook scholarships.

UCLA COURSE READER PROJECT

In fact, several years earlier, the UCLA Library itself had started a partnership that decreased the cost of course materials in a specific format. In 2008, representatives from the undergraduate student government contacted senior administrators to discuss whether the UCLA Library could help lower the prices of course readers and increase access to their contents. Library staff analyzed a selection of readers provided by the students and found that a significant portion of their contents came from UCLA Library–licensed journals and from library-owned books.

With this information, administrators immediately approached the campus store's academic publishing operation, which produces readers on a cost-recovery basis. Store staff explained that a significant portion of the price of each reader came from permissions fees paid to a copyright clearing house on behalf of publishers, which amounted to as much as 60 percent of a reader's cost.

Library administrators quickly realized that because core educational uses across campus are negotiated into its journal license terms, the store could use articles from those journals in readers without paying permissions fees. When store staff recalculated the prices of the readers provided by the students without those fees, they found cost savings as high as 63 percent per reader.[5] As a result, since 2008, checking readers' contents against UCLA Library–licensed resources has become a routine part of the academic publishing operation's workflow, and the library receives a credit line on the cover of each reader for the amount of money these licenses save the purchaser.[6]

THE PILOT INITIATIVE

A funding opportunity also coincided with the library's 2012 discussion about textbook costs. The California Digital Library, which among other services coordinates collective journal licensing on behalf of all University of California campuses, decided to pilot an open access (OA) publishing fund. It offered each campus $10,000, to be matched by the campus, to cover article processing charges in open access journals for UC faculty and researchers. Each campus library would administer its own funds, setting eligibility, application, and award criteria. At the end of the pilot, a report would be issued to help the system and individual campuses determine the scope of the need and the feasibility of operating such a fund on an ongoing basis.

Conversations between UCLA Library senior administrators and senior campus research administrators about the proposed OA publishing fund pilot revealed a low level of interest. Their discussions centered on the fact that a sum of $20,000 would make a maximum of twenty UCLA-authored articles open access, and most of those would be by authors in the sciences, where grant and departmental funding for OA publishing fees already exists.

That's when the lightbulb started to come on: that same amount of money devoted to an open textbook program could potentially save hundreds of students thousands of dollars. The economic argument was compelling. But why should the library, rather than another administrative unit on campus, take on the cost of course materials? As discussions continued, the answer became obvious: collections.

The UCLA Library has more than 12,000,000 print and electronic volumes, provides access to nearly 160,000 journal titles, and holds millions of rare and unique special collections items. It builds these ever-expanding collections to support teaching and research on campus, but aside from the use of selected items in course reserves, the library had scant evidence of how closely aligned those collections were with instructional needs. By working directly with faculty to incorporate collections, services, and expertise into courses, the library could potentially save students money, ensure that it acquired and made accessible materials needed for instruction, and more fully integrate its services into the university's educational mission.

With this realization, the pilot phase of the Affordable Course Materials Initiative (ACMI) began to take shape. The question of how to define the word *textbook* didn't need to be answered. The initiative would operate using the broader conception of "course materials," which would encompass a variety of educational resources including open textbooks, library-licensed or -owned materials in print or digital format, reformatted special collections items, and learning objects and text that faculty create themselves.

A more important question then emerged: would any faculty be willing to work with the library to revamp their course materials? What would engage their interest? From the program at UMass Amherst came an idea: offer grants to get instructors' attention. With that, the final pieces fell quickly into place.[7]

Applicants were eligible for $1,000 grants for courses with enrollments of fewer than 200 students and $2,500 for courses with more than 200 students.[8] Each applicant had to be the instructor of record, and courses needed to be for enrolled undergraduate or graduate students; the only exclusion was UCLA Extension courses.

The application form was kept deliberately short, with only four planning questions: whether the applicant already had ideas on how to revamp the existing course materials; had identified specific library services or resources needed; anticipated any challenges in finding new course materials, teaching with them, or students using them; and could provide intended learning objectives outcomes and potential cost savings. To gather more information, all applicants would also be required to attend an in-person workshop. A small faculty committee would help library administrators decide which applications would receive awards. And program endorsements were sought from influential campus leaders, including the UCLA Office of the Executive Vice Chancellor and Provost and the UCLA Academic Senate.

All faculty members received the initial e-mail announcement and invitation to apply in March 2013. Library administrators held their collective breath waiting to see if anyone would be interested and were surprised and delighted by the quick, positive response: a total of twenty applications arrived in that first wave.[9]

Other developments were equally pleasant surprises, such as the workshop turning into a session in which, after library staff described relevant collections and services, applicants shared ideas and information and brainstormed with one another. And from the faculty review committee came suggestions of two valuable enhancements: a $5,000 grant for particularly complex and far-reaching proposals, and nonmonetary collection development awards. As the committee members observed of the latter, even though that award didn't offer direct funds to recipients, the award letter itself could be useful in early-career faculty members' tenure and promotion packets or job applications. And through these collection development awards, the library acquired materials it knew would be used in specific courses.

During its first year, the pilot attracted applications from twenty-four individuals in twenty-one different academic departments across campus. Eleven applicants were in arts and humanities departments, six were in the social sciences, five were in the health and life sciences, two were in physical sciences and engineering, and two were in law. Thirteen applicants were ladder faculty: five professors, three associate professors, and four assistant professors, plus one professor emeritus. Of the remaining eleven, seven were lecturers, two were adjuncts, one was an instructor, and one was an academic coordinator. The majority of the courses were for undergraduate students: twelve lower division and ten upper division, and two nursing courses combined undergraduate and graduate students. Three were graduate courses, two of which were in the School of Law.

Most, though not all, applicants received awards. Twenty-three awards were given to a total of twenty-two individuals; one applicant received two. Four applications were not awarded for varying reasons: one course was taught before the program's launch date, one applicant had more deserving applications, and the needs of two applicants as well as the possible support the library could provide were unclear.

It quickly became clear that the best approach to each awarded course was to build a team. One librarian served as each grantee's liaison, discussing his or her needs in greater detail, suggesting solutions, coordinating implementation, and gathering feedback. That liaison identified which library experts would be needed for the project; those individuals might include subject specialists, intellectual property specialists, acquisitions staff, digitization technicians, and special collections curators. Although this team-based approach may at first glance appear to be staff-intensive, it actually had the opposite effect: by spreading out the work required on each awarded course across a number of people, each staff member could support more awards.

The projects that applicants proposed varied widely. Perhaps the largest in scope was a three-quarter[10] required English sequence, for which the instructor wanted to develop a digital portal that would facilitate access to trans-Atlantic texts written from before 1700 to the present. Another broad proposal was a project to find or develop an open access platform for an OA statistics textbook that instructors in many disciplines could customize, choosing from discipline-specific learning modules, audiovisual contents, data, and student activities. More straightforward were projects to replace existing texts with library-licensed or -owned texts, improve lab content by adding online resources, and build out class lecture notes into more comprehensive texts.

Not all proposals were successfully implemented, for reasons ranging from the simple to the complex. The OA statistics textbook was never created because the applicant left UCLA the following quarter for a position at another university. However, the concept of a flexible OA textbook publishing platform that facilitates instructor customization remains an intriguing one, and ACMI librarians and staff continue to scout for such an option.

The project to create a portal for the required English sequence encountered more substantive challenges. Its scope was grand: it would be built by UCLA's Center for the Digital Humanities, and instructors, teaching assistants, and librarians would populate it with both library-owned or -licensed and publicly available resources. However, obtaining consensus on course materials among the numerous instructors who teach the sequence proved difficult, and the information technology aspect shifted focus when it was incorporated into a broader proposal from the English Department to a major funder. Instead, as a practical interim solution that offered instructors a single point of access to a variety of materials, several UCLA librarians collaborated to develop an online guide listing collected resources, designed for use by both instructors and students.

Since the initiative was in its pilot phase, these unsuccessful projects were regarded as learning opportunities and data points rather than setbacks. They were balanced by successful projects ranging from the routine to the creative. More routine examples include licensing online access to the text of plays to replace student-purchased paperback copies for a theater course, and digitizing assigned philosophy readings contained in library-owned materials, then helping the instructor post them on UCLA's course management system instead of requiring a course reader.[11]

A more creative approach was developed by the instructor of an ecology and evolutionary biology course required of all students in the major. He replaced two textbooks and a course reader with what he described as a classic/current approach: pairing classic papers from the scientific literature with recently published papers in the same area, all from library-licensed journals and databases, in order to give his students historical perspective and also connect them with cutting-edge research. At the end of the course, he sent ACMI managers a copy of his students' course evaluations; most appreciated the approach and relished the opportunities it afforded for intellectual engagement with the readings, while a few were intimidated by the primary research articles and would have preferred the "known comfort" of a textbook.[12] His conclusion was that a brief study guide would most likely be useful to students in the latter category when he taught the course again.

After a full year, library administrators began to assess the pilot. The library gave a total of $27,500 in monetary grants, out of the previously described total of $30,000 it had secured in pilot funding, and spent an additional $3,792 from the collections budget on acquisitions. A total of 1,742 students were enrolled in awarded courses. These students saved a cumulative total of more than $178,000 over the cost of course materials during the previous quarter when each course was taught, which works out to savings of nearly $100 per student. Qualitative assessments from both instructors and students revealed satisfaction with course materials and student achievement in most awarded courses.

Answers to some of the initial questions began to emerge, along with a number of challenges. As suspected, it quickly became clear that the term *textbook* doesn't resonate widely at UCLA; course materials typically include some combination of multiple books, lab supplies, course readers, data sets, audio and/or video, special collections items (physical or digital), and much more. In addition, instructors for a given course change from quarter to quarter and year to year; they often don't use previous instructors' course materials, as allowed by the university's academic freedom policies.

Though technology offers some opportunities, it also presents obstacles. Not all classrooms have the same technology for presentation and capture, and what is there may not accommodate specialized needs, so audiovisual materials prepared for one course taught in one classroom may not work in subsequent quarters in other classrooms. Perhaps more impactful is the fact that the level of instructional technology understanding, utilization, and support varies widely across campus, with a small centralized office spread thin providing a number of programs and services.

Finally, the sheer scale of the potential need is daunting. More than 3,000 tenure-track faculty and thousands more lecturers teach thousands of courses each year, supported by a library staff of less than 100 librarians and approximately 200 full-time employees.

However, the major impact the initiative had during its brief pilot period made the library's decision an easy one: the initiative became a formal part of its service portfolio as of fall 2015.

RELAUNCH AS A FORMAL SERVICE

To increase ACMI's impact, managers have adopted a more strategic approach upon its relaunch. Open calls for applications continue to be issued annually, but efforts increasingly focus on identifying and targeting high-value courses: those with high enrollments, required in popular majors, taught every quarter, or using the most expensive course materials. Information from the library's reserves program is providing valuable information; large-enrollment courses with high levels of usage of reserves materials are potential high-value candidates for initiative projects.

More information is being gathered about which majors have the most expensive course materials overall, which departments require all instructors for a given course to use the same course materials, and which courses use UCLA instructors' own texts. Research is being done to learn how instructors choose course materials, how they interact with publishers' sales representatives, and what role academic department administrators play in the process. Work needs to be put into persuading instructors to use their colleagues' course materials developed with ACMI awards and into persuading ACMI recipients to adopt an ACMI-like approach to course materials in other courses they teach.

Broader engagement with the OER community has provided program administrators with valuable contextual information and a welcome sense of a shared goal, but with very few tangible solutions that will help the UCLA Library as it expands the initiative. Many of the OER movement's most noteworthy success stories have come from settings where it was a relatively simple, straightforward matter of replacing an expensive textbook on a subject with an open textbook on the same subject. The most successful OER programs appear to be at community colleges and four-year colleges where each course uses one or just a few standard texts, and departments mandate their use in that course regardless of instructor.

Much of the OER community's activity has also focused on quantity—that is, creating more OERs—and there are now an impressive number of repositories and titles. But relatively little work has focused on discoverability—that is, how instructors can quickly find just the right OER when it's needed. Comments from colleagues, including traffic on OER discussion lists and anecdotes heard at conferences, reinforce this impression, with constant pleas for recommendations of textbooks and supporting materials in various subject areas.

Even less work in the OER community has focused on the human factor—that is, absent an institutional or legislative mandate, how to convince individual instructors that adopting different course materials is worth the time it will take to revamp curricula and that the new materials will be of high quality. The complexity of the instructional environment at UCLA and similar universities just in terms of the diversity of materials for each course is daunting. Add to this faculty freedom of choice, and the challenge becomes even more immense.

Where does that leave libraries at research universities—should they embrace the OER movement? When it comes to its goals of accessibility and affordability, the answer is a resounding "yes." It's just the approach and methods that may need tweaking in more complex institutions.

A straightforward, plug-and-play approach taken by a community college most likely won't work at a research-intensive institution. For example, simply finding an open textbook on introductory psychology, then asking an instructor who teaches a course in that area to use it is unlikely to succeed.

However, the good news is that this presents research libraries with a major opportunity. At a research university, where library collections are significant and library expertise in providing instructional services is broad-based, the library is the most logical home for programs to reduce the cost of course materials. Such programs increase the value and visibility of the library, more fully integrate the library into the day-to-day life of students and faculty, and offer appealing options for attracting donor support.

Libraries that haven't yet dipped a toe into textbook affordability may wonder how and where to start. The UCLA Library's experiences suggest that you can start anywhere; just keep a few things in mind:

> One size may not fit all, but there may be a few sizes that fit many. The more libraries that launch programs to address the costs of course materials, the more models other libraries will have to consider. Look at what your peer institutions are doing, and see if any of their programs, or parts of those programs, will work on your campus.

Legislation, policies, and programs focused on "textbooks" won't achieve results in all contexts. Don't sit back and wait for them to make a significant impact at your institution—but by all means support them and leverage them as best you can.

Concentrating on quantity over discoverability, on one-for-one substitutions rather than uniqueness, makes that one size fit even fewer. Don't start your efforts by looking at what open textbooks are available; start with your instructors. Understand their needs, what they teach with, and where that intersects with your library's collections, services, and expertise.

As course materials, many instructors use their own or their colleagues' journal articles and book chapters, to which they signed away educational reuse rights when they signed the publication agreements. Work with your faculty to publish in OA journals, negotiate publication agreements to retain their educational reuse rights, post their scholarship in OA repositories, and support other OA efforts as appropriate.

Don't judge your efforts by the results achieved at other institutions. It's difficult not to be envious of others' success, but remember that not all higher education environments are the same. The results may be slower to come on your campus or may not be as spectacular in terms of dollar savings, but any savings will be appreciated by the students. And don't forget that the educational achievement results and closer relationships with instructors and academic departments are also vitally important.

Don't be daunted by the size of the task; just find a place to start, and be flexible, changing course as needed.

It may sound counterintuitive, but the UCLA Library's long-term goal for its Affordable Course Materials Initiative is that it disappears. There will be no need for incentives to attract instructors' attention because all librarians will routinely work hand in hand with instructors on their course materials, identifying, acquiring, or digitizing items as necessary. As a matter of course, all instructors will consider the cost of assigned materials; actively revamp curricula in order to utilize UCLA Library collections, lower costs, and increase access; and coordinate efforts department-wide so that all students in a given course, regardless of instructor, use the same materials. Technological capabilities will align with instructional needs and instructors' capabilities to facilitate both access to and the creation of new course materials.

Make it your goal to create such a successful program on your campus that eventually it disappears—then there won't be just one size. There will be an infinite number of programmatic approaches of sizes and scopes and contents of course materials that fit every course, every instructor, and every student. Our libraries, our universities, and our collective knowledge will be the richer for it.

Notes

1. Pell Grants are based on "exceptional need." Unlike loans, they do not need to be repaid; for more financial aid demographic information, see www.ucla.edu/about/facts-and -figures.
2. For the 2016–17 academic year, the estimate has risen to $1,635. See www.admission .ucla.edu/prospect/budget.htm.
3. The original plan was developed by a team appointed by the State Board of Education and the University of California Board of Regents in 1960, and legislation was passed to implement parts of it shortly thereafter. The plan has subsequently been revised several times. For more information, see www.ucop.edu/acadinit/mastplan/.
4. The UMass Amherst Libraries' program is called the Open Education Initiative; see www.library.umass.edu/services/teaching-and-learning/oer/open-education-initiative. The Temple Libraries' program is the Alternate Textbook Project; see http://guides .temple.edu/alttextbook.
5. The savings ranged from twelve cents per reader to $30.18 each.
6. Unfortunately, not all students benefit from this ongoing partnership because some faculty members have their readers produced by off-campus, commercial copy shops, which aren't covered by the library's license terms.
7. The program's initial funding totaled $30,000: $10,000 from the California Digital Library, $10,000 from the UCLA Library, and $10,000 from the UCLA Office of the Executive Vice Chancellor and Provost. The UCLA Library obtained permission from the California Digital Library to repurpose its open-access publishing fund allocation for this pilot.
8. The modest yet significant sums offer instructors an incentive for the time it takes to identify new resources, adjust syllabi, and modify assignments and can be used to cover any actual expenses. They are transferred to recipients' academic departments and can be used for any pedagogical purposes allowed by the departments.
9. A total of twenty-six applications were submitted by twenty-four individuals during the initial one-year pilot phase.
10. UCLA is on the quarter system.

11. The system is password-protected, and each course's site is open only to students enrolled in that course.
12. Individual names were redacted.

Bibliography

"The Alternative Textbook Project at Temple University Libraries." Temple University (LibGuide). http://guides.temple.edu/alttextbook.

"Facts and Figures." University of California at Los Angeles. www.ucla.edu/about/facts-and-figures.

"Fees, Tuition, and Estimated Student Budget." University of California at Los Angeles. www.admission.ucla.edu/prospect/budget.htm.

"Master Plan for Higher Education in California." University of California: Office of the President. www.ucop.edu/acadinit/mastplan/.

"UMass Library Open Education Initiative." UMass Amherst Libraries (LibGuide). www.library.umass.edu/services/teaching-and-learning/oer/open-education-initiative.

2

CURRICULUM-DRIVEN ACQUISITIONS

The University of Arizona Libraries' Evolving Role in Campus Materials Support

Jim Martin and Niamh Wallace

Textbooks and other monographs assigned for courses pose unique challenges for those who manage collections in academic libraries. While students clearly have a need for these materials and may expect that the library will make them available, many academic libraries have collection development and interlibrary loan policies which specifically exclude "textbooks" from their scope. The reasons provided for the exclusion often point to a library's budgetary limitations, staffing issues and costs related to maintaining a print reserve textbook collection, an inability to keep print textbooks on the shelf, and the frequency with which textbooks issue new editions.

Recently, however, academic libraries are reconsidering long-held assumptions about their role in providing textbooks for their users. A panel at the 2014 Charleston Library Conference, for example, addressed the "evolving landscape of course content, specifically textbooks," and the new opportunities for libraries wanting to help reduce the cost of education for the students they serve.[1] This is also evidenced by the increase in the number of libraries now involved to various degrees in projects similar to the one we describe here.[2]

While traditional textbooks for the most part remain unavailable in an e-book format to academic libraries, the publishing environment is constantly changing. This evolution of e-books and their associated licenses, open educational resources, and other experiments to develop low-cost course materials has also changed the landscape in terms of what libraries are able to reasonably offer to students and faculty.

The high price of textbooks is also a very public issue, seen as part of a trend of increasing costs of higher education in general, and has received a great deal of attention on campuses nationwide. According to a report by the National Association of College Stores, "While the prices of new textbooks rise faster than the CPI [consumer price index], student per capita spending on learning content is declining. Students rent new and used books; buy used, older, or foreign editions; use (legal and illegal) download sites; or borrow course materials. Some simply disregard faculty assignments."[3] Subsequently, with the advent of new models of e-book licensing and OER opportunities, libraries have stepped in to assume a leadership role in helping alleviate these pressures for students. This is emerging as an important strategy for libraries wanting to contribute more directly to broader campus efforts related to student success and retention. It is also part of a larger shift in libraries toward building collections that are in alignment with the curriculum, rather than solely research.

REQUIRED COURSE MATERIALS AT THE UNIVERSITY OF ARIZONA

The Higher Education Opportunity Act (HEOA) of 2008 includes a provision that requires textbook information to be available as part of the class schedule when students register. At the University of Arizona (UA), the Arizona Board of Regents has also mandated that information about required course materials must be submitted to the UA Bookstore prior to the start of each semester, including summer and winter sessions.[4]

To assist with this process, the UA Bookstore sets four deadlines during the year for faculty to submit their lists of required course materials for the upcoming semester or intersession. This information is then disseminated to students, who may log in to their campus account and view information about the materials assigned for the courses they have registered for. For many years, the UA Bookstore has also provided students with numerous options for obtaining access to their textbooks. Information is provided on the cost and availability of print editions at the UA Bookstore, and various options are provided for the purchase or rental of electronic editions from a variety of providers.

As a note of clarification, we use "required course materials" to refer to any text that faculty instruct their students to purchase for course use, including both titles that would be categorized as traditional textbooks, and produced explicitly for the educational market, as well as other works that are not defined as such. In this way, the term is synonymous with "textbook," as it is understood in the general sense by faculty, students, and the bookstore.

In 2012, the UA Libraries (UAL) approached the UA Bookstore to propose a pilot project in which the required course materials lists compiled by the bookstore could be reviewed by the UAL for current holdings and potential purchase. This information would subsequently be shared with faculty by UAL and pushed out to students through the campus's course management system. Due to the nature of how these materials would be used, and the lack of a print reserve service at the UAL, only e-book editions with multiple-user options were considered. It was decided that faculty for whom the UAL could make available any of their required course materials for the upcoming semester would be contacted with a personalized e-mail, noting the course[s], and providing direct links to the titles in the UAL catalog.

To date, the project has reviewed lists for twelve semesters and intersessions. On average, we have been able to provide access to 16 percent of the total textbook adoption requests submitted by faculty each semester, impacting an average of 254 courses a semester and totaling an average of $456,711 in potential savings each semester (figure 2.1).

Our workflow, although continually refined, is still a largely manual process, involving three UAL departments: liaison librarians in Research & Learning, acquisitions staff, and our web development team. A few weeks after the textbook adoption deadline, the UA Bookstore sends us a spreadsheet listing course, instructor, enrollment, and required course material title. Typically, these files include an average of 2,000 titles, listed with their print ISBNs. UAL acquisitions staff review the lists and identify multiuser e-books that we own or can purchase. Once the searching process is complete and e-books available through the library are identified, three outputs are generated: (1) e-books are embedded in the campus course management system for each affected course, (2) links on the textbook purchase options list on the bookstore's website are

SEMESTER	LIST TOTAL	E-BOOKS THROUGH LIBRARY	PERCENTAGE OF TOTAL (%)	COURSES	STUDENTS	SAVINGS ($)
Spring 2016	1,975	337	17	259	9,126	541,883
Fall 2015	1,954	302	15	243	7,737	385,028
Spring 2015	1,711	241	14	208	6,961	322,753
Fall 2014	2,202	378	17	308	9,904	577,181

Figure 2.1 | **Percentage of Total Textbook Adoption Requests Available as Library E-Books and Potential Savings**

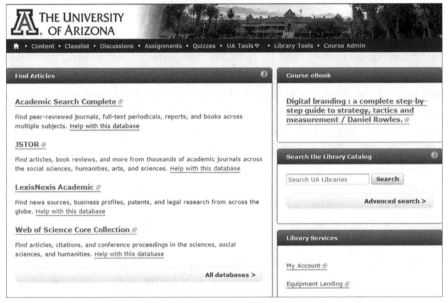

Figure 2.2 | **View of Course E-book in Course Management System**

populated with course e-books, if available, and (3) e-mails are sent to individual faculty notifying them of e-book availability.

UAL has developed a point of integration with the campus course management system (D2L), known as the Library Tools Tab. The Library Tools Tab is the result of a long collaboration with the campus department that manages D2L, and represents an effort to offer scalable access to library resources tailored to the department, course, or even course section level.[5] The Library Tools Tab was seen as an obvious home for these e-books, as it provides easy access to required reading in the space where students are actively completing coursework (figure 2.2). Since the library began embedding course e-books

Figure 2.3 | **Student Booklist View on Bookstore's Website, Showing Link to Check Library E-Book Availability**

into the Library Tools Tab for relevant courses, we've seen overall views of the Library Tools Tab increase 83 percent.

The Bookstore Linker is another fruitful outcome from our partnership with the bookstore. Our respective programming staff worked together to place an access point to library-available course materials in the student booklist view on the bookstore's website, enabling students to see the library e-book as an option (if available) at the point of purchase. The link appears on every textbook listing, and checks against a database populated by e-books provided as part of the project (figure 2.3).

If time allows, UAL programming staff generate e-mail templates, auto-populated with specific course, e-book, and licensing information, which individual liaisons can then send on to faculty to notify them about available library e-books. A PHP script generates e-mail files from a template. The script reads from an Excel spreadsheet that lists the e-book title, instructor, and liaison librarian as determined by the course prefix for each course. The script moves the e-mail file into a liaison-labeled folder, and each liaison can open and send the pre-populated e-mails from their e-mail address (figure 2.4).

In some cases, when time was an issue, we've had to send generic e-mails to relevant faculty alerting them to visit the Library Tools Tab in their D2L course pages to see available e-books. It is important to note that faculty are always informed that print copies will continue to be available for purchase by their students at the UA Bookstore.

TO: [Course Instructor]

FROM: [Librarian]

SUBJECT: Course E-Books available through UA Library Catalog

BODY:

Dear Professor,

The UA Libraries are pleased to be able to provide your students with free access to the following ebook(s), which you requested for your course(s) SOC 307 for Fall 2014:

> CLIMATE OF INJUSTICE; http://sabio.library.arizona.edu/
> record=b5544257~S9; Unlimited User

These ebooks are also linked to your D2L or Blackboard course page in the Library Tools tab.

All of the titles you requested (including those listed above) will continue to remain available for purchase by your students through the UA BookStore http://uabookstore.arizona.edu/, should they prefer to have (or you require that they have) their own copy.

If you have any questions about the course materials through the UA Library catalog, please feel free to contact me with any questions at [librarian]@[institution].edu.

Sincerely,

[Librarian]

Figure 2.4 | **Pre-Populated E-Mails Generated for Faculty**

ISSUES AND CHALLENGES

Impact on Budget

As noted earlier, textbooks have commonly been excluded from traditional collection development policies. This is the case at the UAL, where set parameters on both our patron-driven acquisitions and approval plans block the addition of formally designated "textbooks" to our catalog and/or physical collection. Our interlibrary loan policy also excludes this category of material from being borrowed. One of the initial concerns around the course materials project was that it would send a mixed message to campus about the UAL policy on acquiring textbooks. For the most part, however, that has not occurred. This is primarily due to two reasons: first, it turns out that many of the materials on the list of required course materials are not classified as textbooks. Second, the vast majority (approximately 85 percent) of materials on the lists are not even available for academic libraries to license in a multiuser e-book format (figure 2.1). While there is some evidence that textbooks may become more widely available to academic libraries—for example, over 1,000 textbooks published by the Cambridge University Press are now available to libraries for a flat fee of $500 each[6]–we have not observed any dramatic changes in expenditures over the course of this project. For the most part, standard commercial textbooks assigned in courses must be purchased or rented by individuals.[7]

A second concern was that, with over 2,000 titles on the lists each semester, the impact on UAL's information resources budget would make this project unsustainable. But in fact the annual cost to UAL has ranged between $25,000 and $30,000 each year of the project, an amount easily absorbed by the overall savings on monographs realized by UAL after moving to an almost entirely patron-driven acquisition model for our monographs.[8] The percentage of titles on the lists that are available for purchase by the UAL each semester remains fairly consistent, as have expenditures.

E-Book Licenses and User Expectations

During the first few semesters of the project, e-books with single users or very limited concurrent users were included in the scope of materials we would acquire. However, we quickly learned that there were simply too many problems created when the demand for the e-book outstripped the license terms. We have since only acquired and promoted to faculty and students those required course materials for which we can assure no turnaways or very few turnaways. One development which has helped in this regard is the establishment of nonlinear lending and other unlimited user license models. Also, for certain platforms with limited concurrent users, additional access is automatically purchased by the UAL when the use limit is reached, and the process is seamless for our users. In the early days of the project, there was very little to no information about the license terms for the e-books, either in our catalog records or in the e-book platforms themselves, and this led to inquiries from both faculty and students regarding the availability of the titles for those enrolled in the course. For this reason, the landing page for our Bookstore Linker, before routing users directly to the e-book, lists concurrent use license terms in a user-friendly manner (figure 2.5). As time has progressed, this has become less of an issue, as vendors are supplying licensing information in e-book catalog records, and the user interfaces of many large e-book platforms now display licensing information as well.

Aside from the lack of clear license terms, the usability of many e-book platforms has surfaced as a concern, thanks to pervasive digital rights management (DRM) that overlays many of the e-books in the main aggregators. A recent study has shown that students are often frustrated by e-book use limitations, and heavily prefer the ability to print or save portions or the entirety of the book in PDF, a format they are familiar with.[9] As part of this project, we have not restricted our purchasing criteria to only include DRM-free e-books, although it has been a point of discussion. The majority of the e-books provided are from four major platforms: Myilibrary, ebrary, EBL, and EBSCOhost—all of which are restricted by some level of DRM.

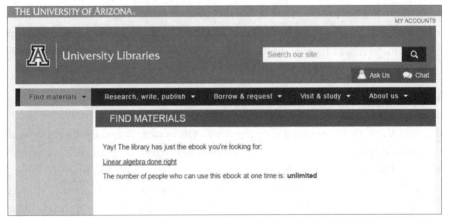

Figure 2.5 | **Landing Page from Bookstore Linker**

Workflow

Legitimate concerns remain about how much staff time is required to process the required course materials lists throughout the year, and to complete all the steps necessary to acquire and promote the materials in a timely manner, as described previously. While improvements have been made over time, there is still an appreciable amount of staff and librarian time required for the project to be successful. By far, the most time-consuming part of the workflow is searching the list to identify e-books either owned or available for purchase. It takes three acquisitions staff members roughly a month to search each ISBN in our book vendor databases to identify e-books in our holdings, as well as purchase those with appropriate licenses when possible. Verifying access to purchased e-books is also part of this process. Often, we are only able to alert faculty to the availability of a course-specific library e-book mere days before the beginning of the semester. We are currently exploring a model that would spread out the workflow over a longer period of time, to the benefit of project partners as well as end users.

FUTURE PLANS

To address the major concerns indicated above, we have two main objectives for the project heading into our fifth year: finding ways to automate as much of the workflow as possible, and reducing the bottleneck that results from processing long lists by requesting compiled adoption lists for each semester in sequences, rather than at once. We also have plans to gather data that could help us identify any correlation between our efforts and student success, instructional efficiency, or reducing the overall cost of enrollment. Specifically, we would like to gauge how aware students are of library-supplied e-book options (where they exist), and what impact this has on their decision to purchase or rent their own personal print or digital copies of these materials. This type of impact could be illustrated by more in-depth feedback from students in these courses and their instructors or by demonstrating appreciable use, such as through e-book use statistics originating from specific D2L course pages. There are many recent studies that examine the experience of students who use e-textbooks.[10] They suggest both the potential that e-textbooks have for students, and where they continue to fall short of their expectations.

Beyond the immediate scope of the project, UAL continues to develop its strategy to encourage faculty to consider the adoption of low/no-cost textbooks and OER. Toward this end, UAL plans to explore how we could become more appropriately sequenced and embedded in the campus textbook adoption process. By doing so, we believe we could make library-owned course materials available to students in a timelier way, and also use this interaction to offer faculty suggestions for potential alternatives to costly textbooks and other course materials. The UAL Strategic Plan has identified this project as one of its top priorities, so we will be pursuing these opportunities in the coming year and working to make significant progress in this area.

Notes

1. Nicole Allen, Charles Lyons, and Bob Nardini, "From Course Reserves . . . to Course Reversed? The Library's Changing Role in Providing Textbook Content" (2014), Proceedings of the Charleston Library Conference, http://dx.doi.org/10.5703/1288284315617.

2. "Course Textbooks (E-Books) Available at Kennedy Library," California Polytechnic State University, www.lib.calpoly.edu/search-and-find/open-resources/required-text books; Patrick L. Carr, James D. Cardin, and Daniel L. Shouse, "Aligning Collections with Student Needs: East Carolina University's Project to Acquire and Promote Online Access to Course-Adopted Texts," *Serials Review* 42, no. 1 (2016): 1–9; "Textbooks Available as E-Books in the Library," San Jose State University, www.library.sjsu.edu/affordable-learning-solutions/textbooks-available-e-books-library; "E-Textbooks for Students," Louisiana State University, www.lib.lsu.edu/e-books; "The E-Textbooks Initiative," State University of New York at Buffalo, www.buffalo.edu/provost/policies-and-resources/efund/1112efunded/etextbooks.html; "E-Textbooks at Atkins Library," University of North Carolina-Charlotte, www.http://atkinsapps.uncc.edu/etextbooks.

3. R. N. Katz and R. Yanosky, *Mapping the Learning Content Ecosystem: An Inquiry into the Disruption, Evolution, and Transformation of the Learning Content Ecosystem* (Oberlin, OH: National Association of College Stores, 2015), 13.

4. "The Federal Higher Education Opportunity Act of 2008," University of Arizona BookStores, www.uabookstores.arizona.edu/heoa.

5. For a history of the development of our course management system integration, see Elizabeth Kline, Niamh Wallace, Leslie Sult, and G. Mike Hagedon, "Embedding the Library in the LMS: Is it a Good Investment for Your Organization's Information Literacy Program?" in *Distributed Learning: Incorporating Online Options into Your Information Literacy Instruction* (Cambridge: Chandos, 2016).

6. "For Librarians—Price List," Cambridge University Press, www.e-books.cambridge.org/user_streaming.jsf?pageId=10332&level=2&pageTitle=Price+List.

7. Charles Lyons and Dean Hendrix, "Textbook Affordability: Is There a Role for the Library?" *The Serials Librarian* 66, no. 1–4 (2014): 262–67.

8. Jason C. Dewland and Andrew See, "Notes on Operations: Patron-Driven Acquisitions: Determining the Metrics for Success," *Library Resources & Technical Services* 59, no. 1 (2015): 13–23.
9. Kendall Hobbs and Diane Klare, "Are We There Yet?: A Longitudinal Look at E-Books through Students' Eyes," *Journal of Electronic Resources Librarianship* 28, no. 1 (2016): 9–24.
10. Ibid.; David James Johnston et al., "Ease of Use and Usefulness as Measures of Student Experience in a Multi-Platform E-Textbook Pilot," *Library Hi Tech* 33, no. 1 (2015): 65–82; Lori Baker-Eveleth and Robert W. Stone, "Usability, Expectation, Confirmation, and Continuance Intentions to Use Electronic Textbooks," *Behaviour & Information Technology* 34, no. 10 (2015): 992–1004.

Bibliography

Allen, Nicole, Charles Lyons, and Bob Nardini. "From Course Reserves ... to Course Reversed? The Library's Changing Role in Providing Textbook Content." 2014. Proceedings of the Charleston Library Conference. http://dx.doi.org/10.5703/1288284315617.

Baker-Eveleth, Lori, and Robert W. Stone. "Usability, Expectation, Confirmation, and Continuance Intentions to Use Electronic Textbooks." *Behaviour & Information Technology* 34, no. 10 (2015): 992–1004. http://dx.doi.org/10.1080/0144929X.2015.1039061.

Carr, Patrick L., James D. Cardin, and Daniel L. Shouse. "Aligning Collections with Student Needs: East Carolina University's Project to Acquire and Promote Online Access to Course-Adopted Texts." *Serials Review* 42, no. 1 (2016): 1–9. http://dx.doi.org/10.1080/00987913.2015.1128381.

Dewland, Jason C., and Andrew See. "Notes on Operations: Patron-Driven Acquisitions: Determining the Metrics for Success." *Library Resources & Technical Services* 59, no. 1 (2015): 13–23. http://dx.doi.org/10.5860/lrts.59n1.13.

Hobbs, Kendall, and Diane Klare. "Are We There Yet?: A Longitudinal Look at E-Books through Students' Eyes." *Journal of Electronic Resources Librarianship* 28, no. 1 (2016): 9–24. http://dx.doi.org/10.1080/1941126X.2016.1130451.

Johnston, David James, Selinda Adelle Berg, Karen Pillon, and Mita Williams. "Ease of Use and Usefulness as Measures of Student Experience in a Multi-Platform E-Textbook Pilot." *Library Hi Tech* 33, no. 1 (2015): 65–82. doi: 10.1108/lht-11–2014–0107.

Katz, R. N., and R. Yanosky. *Mapping the Learning Content Ecosystem: An Inquiry into the Disruption, Evolution, and Transformation of the Learning Content Ecosystem.* Oberlin, OH: National Association of College Stores, 2015.

Kline, Elizabeth, Niamh Wallace, Leslie Sult, and Gregory Mike Hagedon. "Embedding the Library in the LMS: Is it a Good Investment for Your Organization's Information

Literacy Program?" In *Distributed Learning: Incorporating Online Options into Your Information Literacy Instruction.* Cambridge: Chandos, 2016.

Lyons, Charles, and Dean Hendrix. "Textbook Affordability: Is There a Role for the Library?" *The Serials Librarian* 66, no. 1–4 (2014): 262–67. http://dx.doi.org/10.1080/0361526X.2014.877282.

3

THINKING OUTSIDE THE PAGES
The University of North Carolina at Charlotte's Atkins Library E-Textbook Program

Elizabeth Siler

The Atkins Library at the University of North Carolina at Charlotte (UNCC), like many universities across the country, has seen the significant rise in costs that our students pay for their textbooks each year, and believes it is one place the library can make a difference in the ever-increasing cost of higher education for students. Within the literature about textbook costs, students could be spending close to $1,200 per year to meet the reading requirements for their classes.[1] Despite rising tuition and fees, library expenditures as a percentage of total university expenditures have decreased significantly over the past thirty years from 3.7 percent in 1982 to 1.7 percent in 2011.[2] Many libraries may not have the funding or staffing to create open educational resources, or publish local textbooks. The program discussed in this chapter can be implemented at any library and can be tailored to how much or how little the library would like to devote to it.

E-BOOKS AT THE ATKINS LIBRARY

Before diving into the project, it is important to understand the three basic principles that the Atkins Library follows when purchasing e-books:

1. Unlimited simultaneous user access
2. No technical or contractual digital rights management (DRM)
3. Perpetual access and/or archival rights

These principles were developed after years of frustration with single-use, DRM, and subscription-based e-books. The principles are also key to being able to make e-books available as textbooks to classrooms.

THE ATKINS LIBRARY E-TEXTBOOK PROGRAM

The Atkins Library E-Textbook program has two major components to help bring assigned textbooks to the students free of charge. The first component is to review the bookstore list and identify the titles the library has in its collection or can purchase as e-books. The second component is to solicit requests from faculty on e-books they would like to assign as textbooks through the library by providing them with a list of titles the library has or can get from vendors that provide e-books under the three principles of e-book purchasing at the Atkins Library.

The Bookstore List

Obtaining a copy of the bookstore list can sometimes be difficult, depending on who runs the bookstore on campus and how cooperative they are with the library. This type of program can often cut into the bookstore's bottom line, making it less likely they would want to collaborate. At UNCC, as part of library policy, we do not interlibrary loan (ILL) books that have been assigned as textbooks. In order to ensure we are not doing this, we receive the bookstore textbook list and check against the ILL requests. They are happy to provide the list under these circumstances and we are able to use the list for both purposes. The list we receive from the bookstore includes the following information: author, title, publisher, ISBN, professor, class section, class estimated enrollment, and class actual enrollment. Our library uses all of this information to help facilitate the process of identifying titles the library owns or could purchase, notifying faculty of the access, and assessing the number of students who are impacted by the program. To identify titles the library can provide, the list is sorted by publisher, because the library only purchases titles directly from publishers that fit our three basic principles. From this list, I check our holdings. If the title is not in our holdings, I check our vendor's database. Currently, an automatic checking system has not been established.

There are other arguments to be made to the bookstore to convince them to collaborate. First, many universities are making textbook affordability a priority on campus, and by providing the library with the title list for this purpose, it shows a willingness to participate in textbook affordability initiatives. In addition, the majority of the e-books the library can purchase are "course adoption titles," or titles that are not originally published to be used as textbooks, as opposed to traditional textbooks. These titles tend to be lower in cost and are more likely to be purchased on the secondary market. If the bookstore is particularly nervous about the project and is willing to run a pilot with the library, you can review sales of books provided by the library after the end of the semester and determine the effect. At UNCC, we reviewed sales data with the bookstore and found that some students still opted to purchase the print books, even with free access available through the library. This correlates with responses in favor of the print over the e-book format, discovered through a student survey, which will be discussed later in the chapter.

When reviewing the bookstore list, the best way to find the books you are looking for is to sort by publisher. Atkins Library has a limited number of approved publishers/providers to match with titles on the list, avoiding the process of checking access to every single title. In cases where libraries purchase many of their e-books from aggregators, such as ProQuest or EBSCO, that do not meet our three principles, a more systematic approach to reviewing the entire list might be needed because the aggregators provide books for many more publishers than what can be purchased directly.

Faculty Requests

The most unique part of the program comes from giving the faculty the opportunity to use library e-books as textbooks or course adoption titles. We hypothesized that faculty who normally assign e-books as textbooks through the bookstore would also be likely to assign e-books held by the library as textbooks. In addition, we have gotten feedback from faculty that they appreciate the opportunity to assign chapters from several library e-books in order to save students from buying textbooks. The database was created to help encourage our faculty to use the library e-books as part of their course readings, and possibly as the primary source of their required course materials.

The Database

The Faculty Textbook Database contains a list of e-books the library owns or could purchase. The faculty can select to use these titles in their classes by filling out a short form that would be routed to the library for processing and record-keeping purposes. The Atkins Library is fortunate to have a very talented webmaster who worked with the head of Research and Information Services and the collections team to design the interface of the database, which is based on the university bookstore website the faculty currently navigates to request textbooks for each semester.

The Back End

The back end of the database was created in simple SQL and includes the following fields that are shared with the faculty when they search the database. These fields are provided to the library directly from our approved publishers/providers.[3]

Basic Bibliographic Information: The database includes basic bibliographic information including the title, author, and print ISBN. The print ISBN is used because ProQuest Syndetics is used to provide the description information, and the print ISBN is the most accurate match point for Syndetics.

Subject Information: The subject information provided by the publisher/provider is not based on any standard classification, like LC classification. In the beginning, as the database was being built, the collection team tried to normalize the subject areas that each publisher was using, but because the level of specificity varied and there were too many subjects to normalize, we decided to use what the publisher/provider included in its metadata, as is. The subjects are still useful for keyword searching purposes.

URL: The URLs are not visible within the user interface, but come into play upon the selection of materials. In cases where the library already owns the e-book, the URL contains our authentication tool, EZProxy, pre-fix link, which provides a link that faculty and students can use to access the e-book on or off campus. For titles the library already owns, the URL can be sent directly to the faculty member once the title is requested.

Held: In order to indicate to users whether or not we own a title, we use a 0 for not held and a 1 for held.

To keep the information up-to-date within the system, the program administrator will add new title lists to the system periodically, both purchased and newly available for purchase. The system also allows for individual manipulation of title records so the system administrator can, for example, update titles that were previously not owned by the library and were purchased as part of a request through the system.

The Interface

With the back-end information in place, the front end is set up to be easy for faculty to locate and select titles they would like to use in their classes.[4] When a faculty member visits the home page of the database, they see a search box on the right-hand side of the screen which allows the user to search by keyword, which searches the title and the subject fields, author, or ISBN.

Once a search is executed the faculty is presented with the results of the search (see figure 3.1), listing all of the e-books they have to choose from based on the search criteria they entered. If we own the title, there is a green dot next to the Detailed Information link and under the availability column it gives the faculty the option to "Use This," which hyperlinks to the request form. If we

Title	Author(s)	Publisher	Subject(s)	Availability
An End to Global Warming Detailed Information	L.O. Williams	Elsevier	Energy	Request This
Causes, Impacts and Solutions to Global Warming Detailed Information	Ibrahim Dincer, Can Ozgur Colpan, Fethi Kadioglu	Springer	Energy	Use This
Climate Capitalism: Global Warming and the Transformation of the Global Economy Detailed Information	Peter Newell, Matthew Paterson	Cambridge	Earth and Environmental Sciences	Request This

Figure 3.1 | **Search Results in Faculty E-Textbook Database**

do not own the title there is a red dot next to the Detailed Information link and the availability column says "Request This," also hyperlinked.

The links connect the user to a form (see figure 3.2) where they fill out simple information, including Required E-Book Edition (if there are multiple editions), Faculty Name, Faculty E-Mail, the course number, and corresponding semester.

There is also an opportunity to add any special notes for the library, such as how many students are in the class, whether other faculty might be using the same book for another class, or if they would also like a print copy on reserve.

Upon submission of the form, for the "Use This" titles, the system automatically generates the link and provides it on the next screen for the faculty members to use in their classes. If the faculty member chooses a title with the "Request This" link, a message is sent to the library, prompting the process of purchasing the title. It can take between twenty-four hours and two weeks for a title to be purchased, depending on the publisher/provider workflow and

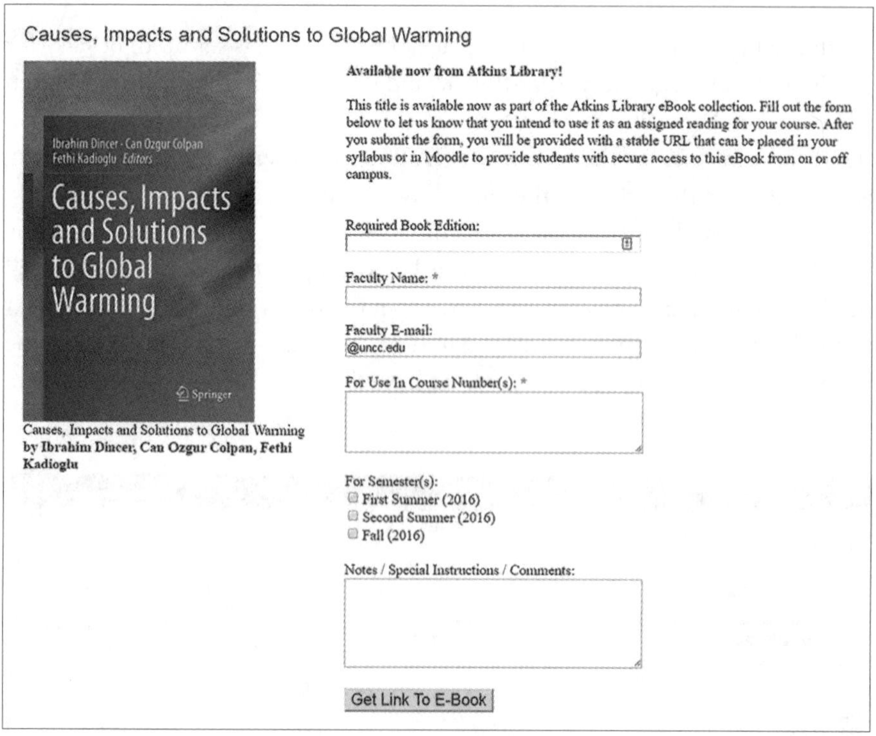

Figure 3.2 | **Faculty Request Form for Library E-Book Adoption**

how often the books are purchased internally. Once the title is available, the library staff sends an e-mail to the faculty member who requested the title with instructions on where a link can be posted for students to access the e-book. In general, book requests are not tracked after the first semester the book is requested. An attempt was made early in the program's inception to contact professors in subsequent semesters after selection, but responses were infrequent and it was determined we did not have the staff time to attend to this task. This information is valuable and if an institution has time and attention to give to this process, it is advisable.

Of course, titles we do own are in the catalog and faculty are welcome to discover and use the titles there, especially considering that all of the e-books the library purchases are optimal for classroom use. The database is part of the marketing plan to encourage faculty to use library e-books as textbooks, as opposed to traditional textbooks, thereby saving students money and increasing the flexibility of the curriculum.

Faculty Outreach

One of the biggest challenges with this project, and other similar projects, is marketing the use of library resources in classes to faculty. The project started with using the textbook list to identify titles already assigned and informing the faculty member of the availability of the title. This process is relatively straight-forward and requires little marketing. Title selection through the database requires faculty to be more proactive, which means the library needs to actively advertise the service. Marketing this product is a delicate process because the library needs to be careful not to shout to the rooftops that the program is a way to replace traditional textbooks, primarily not to damage the relationship we have cultivated with the bookstore.

There are several different ways to approach faculty to encourage them to use the program. Here are several tactics libraries can use to promote this program.

Traditional Marketing

Each semester an e-mail is sent out through the Academic Affairs discussion list, which reaches all full-time teaching faculty, around the same time as deadlines approach for submitting textbook requests through the bookstore. Adjunct faculty are informed of the program through the adjunct faculty website. Faculty are reminded of the program and are encouraged to visit the database as well as consult with the subject librarians on choosing titles to use in their classes. Once this e-mail goes out, subject librarians are instructed to forward the message to their respective departments with their own personalized message to cultivate participation in their areas.

Print marketing can also be an effective tool to get faculty attention, and the library plans to do a large-scale print mailer at the beginning of the semester to engage professors who are more likely to delete or ignore e-mails.

Presentations

As part of the push to increase the use of the program, presentations are given by the collection development librarian to increase awareness. This includes webinars through the Center for Teaching and Learning, presenting the program to the faculty council, and presentations to the faculty who are moving to completely online courses, where e-textbooks can be especially beneficial. Generally, after one of these presentations, requests will come into the system from faculty new to the program. It is preferable to meet with small groups of faculty members, through department meetings and in concert with the library liaison.

Word of Mouth

Many faculty members have discovered the program from other faculty. The key for this to work is for the faculty currently using the program to be happy with the results. The library works hard to make using the program a pleasant and successful experience. One service the library offers is consultations with our library liaisons to help select e-books we can provide as alternatives to traditional textbooks. Librarians will also research other books that are not in the textbook database to determine if there is another way to get the title or possibly license it with a new e-book vendor. The library is also open to contracting to purchase the PDF of an e-book and host it on our secure servers if a vendor is willing to work within those parameters. Information about this type of purchase is addressed in the "Cost to the Library" section below.

Faculty Incentives

Redesigning a class using nontraditional textbooks can be time-consuming for faculty. One method to encourage faculty to take this time is to provide a monetary incentive. It is not a method currently employed in the Atkins Library, but it is a method that has been employed as part of OER initiatives. For example, the University of Massachusetts at Amherst started a program in 2011 to encourage faculty to use OERs as opposed to traditional resources.[5] The university "created an innovative new Open Education grant program in April 2011 that began with 10 $1,000 grants to incentivize faculty who were interested in pursuing alternatives to high cost textbooks."[6]

Program Assessment

With a program like this, which takes considerable time and effort, it is important to continuously assess its success to ensure it is still a viable program and provides value to the campus. Routine assessment also provides insight on future improvement of the program. There are several ways you can assess a program, including looking at general program statistics, usage statistics, and gauging user experience.

General Statistics

The general statistics we gather every semester include the total number of books provided (see figure 3.3), how the books are identified (through bookstore list or the database), the number of students reached, potential student savings, and the cost to the library.

To date, the program at the Atkins Library has been fully implemented for four complete semesters from fall 2014 to spring 2016. The table in figure 3.4 reports the general and usage statistics gathered at the end of each semester. The statistics the library gathers include the total number of e-books used as textbooks, the number of e-books that were identified through the bookstore list, number of e-books requested through the database, number of students

SEMESTER	TOTAL NUMBER OF TEXTBOOKS	TEXTBOOKS ADDED FROM BOOKSTORE LIST	TEXTBOOKS ADDED FROM FACULTY DATABASE	TEXTBOOK EXPENDITURES ($)
Fall 2014	117	62	55	14,193
Spring 2015	158	73	85	4,578
Fall 2015	106	45	62	6,876
Spring 2016	144	92	52	6,431

Figure 3.3 | **Textbook Expenditures by Semester and Method of Selection**

SEMESTER	NUMBER OF STUDENTS	STUDENT SAVINGS ($)	USAGE (FULL-TEXT DOWNLOADS)	COST PER USE ($)
Fall 2014	1,286	137,406.60	5,906	2.40
Spring 2015	2,644	204,703.00	12,123	0.38
Fall 2015	1,763	151,664.46	8,773	0.78
Spring 2016	2,085	224,177.00	14,902	0.43

Figure 3.4 | **Student Savings and Cost per Use by Semester**

in the classes using library e-books as textbooks (students reached), possible student savings, and cost to the library for individual e-book purchases.

There really is not enough data at this point to show patterns of any kind, but there are a few numbers to take note.

Cost to the Library

The cost to the library to run this program is relatively small in comparison to the savings passed on to the students. The average cost of the titles for these e-books is $171. The library does not include titles that cost more than $500 in the database and will only pay more under specific circumstances. For example, for an e-book PDF currently hosted on the library's secure server, the library negotiated to pay an amount to equal the cost of two semesters of students buying the print copy, totaling over $2,500. This particular e-book is projected to be used for up to seven years. Under these circumstances the library might be able to partner with the department the class is under to share the cost. The library is willing to be creative when attempting to provide textbook access to students and will inquire directly with publishers when it appears to be a viable option.

After the first semester the book was purchased, the library does not contact each professor to determine if they plan on using the e-book in future semesters, and so the number of e-books in classes could be much higher than what is reported based on requests each semester. Based on the bookstore textbook list, the library does know that several books purchased in one semester continue to be assigned as textbooks in subsequent semesters, and so the investment in these e-books is cost-effective. As an example of this, the title *Black Feminist Thought* was first purchased by the library for $119 in spring 2014, based on the bookstore list, but before we implemented the database. The title has continued to be assigned every semester since then and the library has provided the textbook at no additional cost to forty-three students, which is a $2 investment per student. This cost will go down further, since the book continues to be assigned.

The purpose of looking at library cost is to show that any library could implement this program at very little cost. If a library did not want to spend additional funds on the program, it could only offer e-books it has purchased through packages as an option to professors. On average, 75 percent of the e-books the library has identified as textbooks come from titles the library currently owns through publisher packages previously purchased.

Student Savings

Another statistic to note is students' savings. These numbers are based on the list price for a new edition through the bookstore or through Amazon and multiplying it by the number of students in each class. As discussed at the beginning of this chapter, textbook affordability is a critical issue on college campuses. Demonstrating that the e-textbook collections save students somewhere between $137,000 and $224,000 each semester can highlight the value of the program, prompting support from upper administration and possibly encouraging more faculty to participate in the program.

Usage Statistics

Based on the four semesters of data collection, the average number of full-text downloads per title (based on COUNTER Compliant Book Report 2 Statistics) is 78 full-text downloads per title. Some of the titles have been used extensively, including one title in the fall of 2015 that was downloaded over 1,729 times. There also have been some titles that have been used very little, or not at all, from both the bookstore list and the titles requested through the database. Extensive inquiry has not been done as to why these e-books that were assigned for a class were not used, but it is something the library plans to review in the future.

The library is able, for the most part, to compare all of our e-book title usage because they are all available as PDF downloads, as opposed to being locked into other proprietary e-readers that do not allow for full-text downloads. The only issue that might arise is how the book is presented in the PDF, either as the full book, or by chapter. Most of the publisher/platforms the library purchases from have PDFs in individual chapters, but there are two exceptions, where one only provides full book downloads, often deflating their usage, and one that provides both full book or individual downloads, which inflates the usage, because when the full book is downloaded, it counts each chapter as an individual download.

User Experience

The general program statistics and the usage statistics can only tell the library so much about a program's success and are of little use without context that can be gained directly from the user. In spring of 2015 the Atkins Library circulated a survey to faculty and students. Three separate surveys were created and dispersed based on the type of participant in the program: students whose class included a textbook from the library (78 respondents out of 2,600 contacted); faculty whose textbook was assigned through the bookstore (19 respondents out of 59 contacted), but was also available through the library; and faculty who used the e-textbook database (18 respondents out of 41 contacted). Although the number of responses was not very high, some information can be gleaned from the responses.

The questions addressed three main points of interest: marketing, user experience, and future use of the program.

Marketing

The questions for each user group varied depending on the type of marketing that was directed to them. For students, we wanted to determine if they knew their textbook was available electronically through the library and, if so, how they heard about it. Our results show that 64 percent of the student respondents were aware of the availability of their textbook through the library, which indicated that more work might need to be done in terms of student outreach. The students learned about their textbooks' electronic availability either directly from their professor, through the library website, or from word of mouth. From these results, shown in in figure 3.5, the library decided to encourage the faculty to make their students aware of the textbooks' availability.

For faculty, the most effective marketing appeared to be e-mail marketing either through an e-mail blast or direct contact from their liaison. All of the faculty who responded to the survey learned about the program through e-mail (see figure 3.6). Although this was supportive of the current marketing plan, the library had not reached out to faculty who had not used the program at all, and

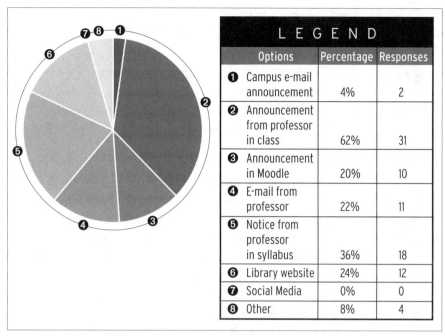

LEGEND		
Options	Percentage	Responses
❶ Campus e-mail announcement	4%	2
❷ Announcement from professor in class	62%	31
❸ Announcement in Moodle	20%	10
❹ E-mail from professor	22%	11
❺ Notice from professor in syllabus	36%	18
❻ Library website	24%	12
❼ Social Media	0%	0
❽ Other	8%	4

Figure 3.5 | **Student Awareness of E-Book Availability of Their Textbook(s)**

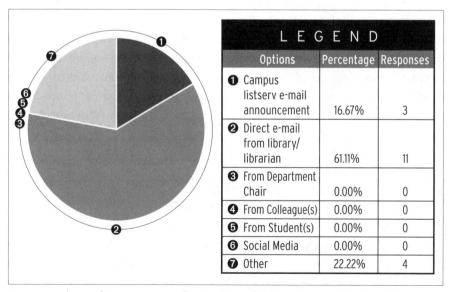

LEGEND		
Options	Percentage	Responses
❶ Campus listserv e-mail announcement	16.67%	3
❷ Direct e-mail from library/ librarian	61.11%	11
❸ From Department Chair	0.00%	0
❹ From Colleague(s)	0.00%	0
❺ From Student(s)	0.00%	0
❻ Social Media	0.00%	0
❼ Other	22.22%	4

Figure 3.6 | **Faculty Awareness of E-Book Availability of Their Textbook(s)**

the library felt it was important to try other strategies, including direct engagement by attending faculty meetings and trainings, and dispersing print fliers.

User Experience

When assessing user experience, there are two experiences to take into account: (1) the use of the program/e-textbook database, and (2) the overall use of the e-book for the course.

The use of the database only applied to the faculty who used the Faculty eTextbook Database to identify e-books to use as textbooks for their course. The survey asked faculty to rate their experience using the database on a scale of 1 to 10, with 10 being the most positive and 1 the least positive. We asked about several database features, including the ability to find e-books, browse topics, the usefulness of the descriptions, and ease of selection. We also asked respondents to rate their experience corresponding with the Atkins Library e-book team, including satisfaction with the confirmation of request, time between request and access, and overall responsiveness. Eighty percent of the respondents rated the database and the team an 8 or higher, which the library considers a success (see figure 3.7).

In addition to the database user experience, we also asked both the students and the professors about their experience using the e-books provided by the library as a textbook (see figures 3.8 and 3.9). The same question was posed to each group: rate from 1 to 10 your experience using the library's e-books, inquiring about several categories including overall use, ease of downloading, keyword searching, printing, saving, and making notes. A majority of the respondents rated each of the experiences a 5 or higher, which is an indication that the e-books were being positively received. For the students, the survey included an additional question inquiring about format preference: the results skewed slightly toward the print format with 41 percent preferring the print, 17 percent preferring the e-book, and 37 percent preferring both. These findings are a little better than what other research suggests about user preference for print books as given in the article "Students' Perceptions of Electronic Textbooks," which states their "findings indicate that students of all ages and experience levels overwhelmingly prefer paper textbooks to electronic textbooks" and "eighty percent of the students in [their] survey would choose a paper textbook over an e-text."[7]

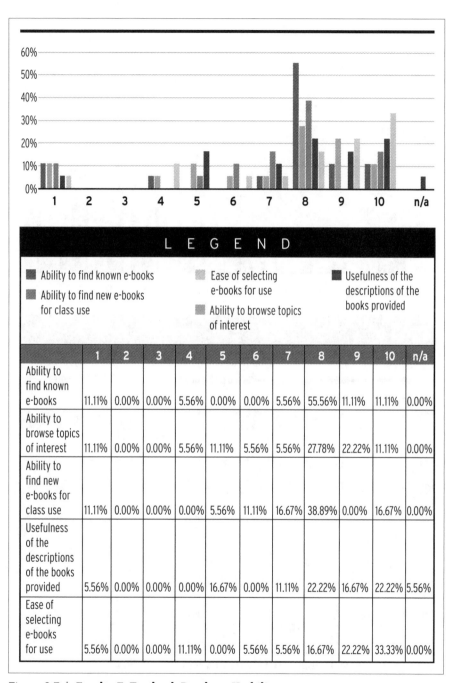

	1	2	3	4	5	6	7	8	9	10	n/a
Ability to find known e-books	11.11%	0.00%	0.00%	5.56%	0.00%	0.00%	5.56%	55.56%	11.11%	11.11%	0.00%
Ability to browse topics of interest	11.11%	0.00%	0.00%	5.56%	11.11%	5.56%	5.56%	27.78%	22.22%	11.11%	0.00%
Ability to find new e-books for class use	11.11%	0.00%	0.00%	0.00%	5.56%	11.11%	16.67%	38.89%	0.00%	16.67%	0.00%
Usefulness of the descriptions of the books provided	5.56%	0.00%	0.00%	0.00%	16.67%	0.00%	11.11%	22.22%	16.67%	22.22%	5.56%
Ease of selecting e-books for use	5.56%	0.00%	0.00%	11.11%	0.00%	5.56%	5.56%	16.67%	22.22%	33.33%	0.00%

Figure 3.7 | **Faculty E-Textbook Database Usability**

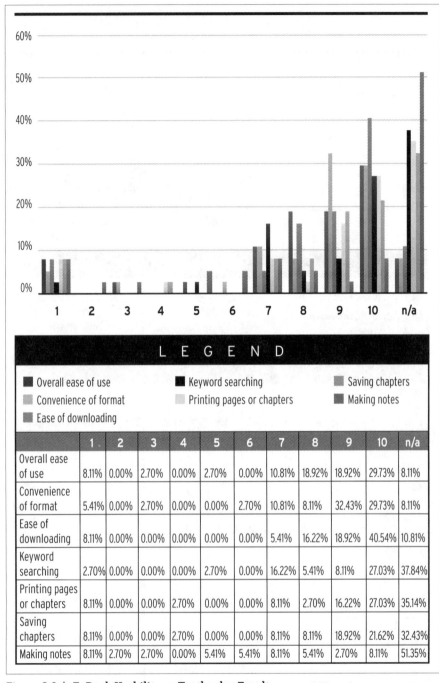

	1	2	3	4	5	6	7	8	9	10	n/a
Overall ease of use	8.11%	0.00%	2.70%	0.00%	2.70%	0.00%	10.81%	18.92%	18.92%	29.73%	8.11%
Convenience of format	5.41%	0.00%	2.70%	0.00%	0.00%	2.70%	10.81%	8.11%	32.43%	29.73%	8.11%
Ease of downloading	8.11%	0.00%	0.00%	0.00%	0.00%	0.00%	5.41%	16.22%	18.92%	40.54%	10.81%
Keyword searching	2.70%	0.00%	0.00%	0.00%	2.70%	0.00%	16.22%	5.41%	8.11%	27.03%	37.84%
Printing pages or chapters	8.11%	0.00%	0.00%	2.70%	0.00%	0.00%	8.11%	2.70%	16.22%	27.03%	35.14%
Saving chapters	8.11%	0.00%	0.00%	2.70%	0.00%	0.00%	8.11%	8.11%	18.92%	21.62%	32.43%
Making notes	8.11%	2.70%	2.70%	0.00%	5.41%	5.41%	8.11%	5.41%	2.70%	8.11%	51.35%

Figure 3.8 | **E-Book Usability as Textbooks: Faculty**

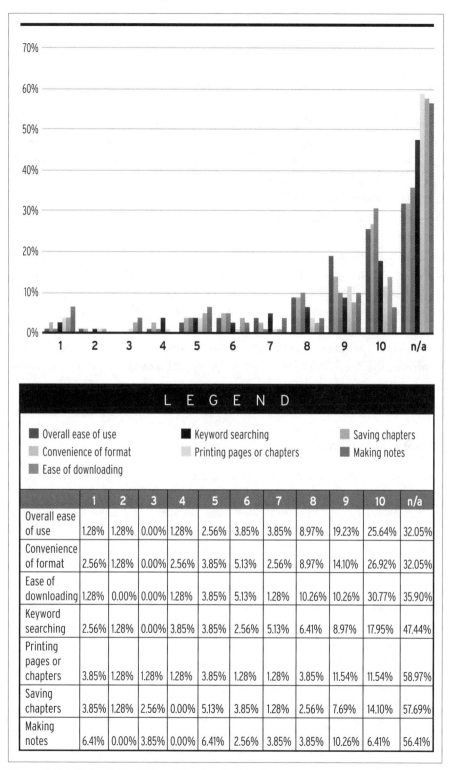

	1	2	3	4	5	6	7	8	9	10	n/a
Overall ease of use	1.28%	1.28%	0.00%	1.28%	2.56%	3.85%	3.85%	8.97%	19.23%	25.64%	32.05%
Convenience of format	2.56%	1.28%	0.00%	2.56%	3.85%	5.13%	2.56%	8.97%	14.10%	26.92%	32.05%
Ease of downloading	1.28%	0.00%	0.00%	1.28%	3.85%	5.13%	1.28%	10.26%	10.26%	30.77%	35.90%
Keyword searching	2.56%	1.28%	0.00%	3.85%	3.85%	2.56%	5.13%	6.41%	8.97%	17.95%	47.44%
Printing pages or chapters	3.85%	1.28%	1.28%	1.28%	3.85%	1.28%	1.28%	3.85%	11.54%	11.54%	58.97%
Saving chapters	3.85%	1.28%	2.56%	0.00%	5.13%	3.85%	1.28%	2.56%	7.69%	14.10%	57.69%
Making notes	6.41%	0.00%	3.85%	0.00%	6.41%	2.56%	3.85%	3.85%	10.26%	6.41%	56.41%

Figure 3.9 | **E-Book Usability as Textbooks: Students**

Future Use

Aside from the predetermined questions, the survey allowed for an open-ended comments section in order to extract additional insight on how the various user groups felt about the program. We received many comments from students and faculty who were appreciative of this no-cost alternative, but who for the most part preferred reading and taking notes within a personal print book. The comments have encouraged the library to explore what can be done to e-books in the future to make them more usable for students and faculty, but still maintain the ability to provide free, unimpeded access to multiple users at one time.

Much of what was learned from the entire survey helped us to determine if the program had a future, but a final question was posed to the faculty, in particular: whether they would use the program in the future. Of the 37 respondents, 36 said yes, which is encouraging and concludes that the program is valuable, at least to the faculty surveyed. The goal now is to encourage faculty to participate, which circles back to the marketing section of this chapter, and reinforces the need for there always to be a continuous effort to maintain the success of the program.

FINAL THOUGHTS

Academic libraries are increasingly being approached by their administration to help with the textbook affordability on their campus. By leveraging and marketing existing and future e-book collections as course adoptions, the program developed at the Atkins Library is something any library can implement no matter how big or small.

Notes

1. Ashely Klair Burke, "Textbook Alternatives: Faculty Approaches to Reducing Student Costs for Required Course Materials," Syracuse University Honors Program Capstone Projects 2014 (May 1, 2014).
2. Phil Davis, "Libraries Receive Shrinking Share of University Expenditures," *Scholarly Kitchen* (blog), July 22, 2014, https://scholarlykitchen.sspnet.org/2014/07/22/libraries-receive-shrinking-share/.
3. Follow updates from the Charlotte Initiative for Permanent Acquisition of E-Books by Academic Libraries at http://charlotteinitiative.uncc.edu/.

4. "Faculty eTextbook Database" (2017), J. Murrey Atkins Library, University of North Carolina at Charlotte, http://library.uncc.edu/et.
5. See chapters 1, 6, and 7 for successful examples of faculty grant programs to promote open educational resources.
6. Marilyn Billings, William M. Cross, Brendan O'Connell, Gregory Raschke, and Charlotte Roh, "Libraries Leading the Way on the Textbook Problem," Proceedings of the Charleston Library Conference 2014 (November 2014): 503–11, doi: 10.5703/1288284315631.
7. Matthew McGowan, Paul Stephens, and Charles West, "Students' Perceptions of Electronic Textbooks," *Issues in Information Systems* 10, no. 2 (2009): 459–65. www.iacis.org/iis/2009/P2009_1299.pdf.

Bibliography

Billings, Marilyn, William M. Cross, Brendan O'Connell, Gregory Raschke, and Charlotte Roh. "Libraries Leading the Way on the Textbook Problem." Proceedings of the Charleston Library Conference 2014 (November 2014): 503–11. doi: 10.5703/1288284315631.

Burke, Ashley Klair. "Textbook Alternatives: Faculty Approaches to Reducing Student Costs for Required Course Materials." Syracuse University Honors Program Capstone Projects 2014 (May 1, 2014). http://surface.syr.edu/honors_capstone/815/.

Davis, Phil. "Libraries Receive Shrinking Share of University Expenditures." *Scholarly Kitchen* (blog), July 22, 2014. https://scholarlykitchen.sspnet.org/2014/07/22/libraries-receive-shrinking-share/.

"Faculty eTextbook Database." J. Murrey Atkins Library, University of North Carolina at Charlotte. http://library.uncc.edu/et.

McGowan, Matthew, Paul Stephens, and Charles West. "Students' Perceptions of Electronic Textbooks." *Issues in Information Systems* 10, no. 2 (2009): 459–65. www.iacis.org/iis/2009/P2009_1299.pdf.

THE BOTTOM LINE
DDA, E-Textbooks, and Student Savings at Louisiana State University Libraries

Alice Daugherty and Emily Frank

ollection development has passed through various trend cycles in academic libraries, with the demand-driven acquisition (DDA) model currently experiencing widespread acceptance and adoption. Also known as patron-driven acquisition, this acquisition strategy moves the purchasing impetus from being "just-in-case"—a model attempting to anticipate user needs, to a "just-in-time"—a point-of-need model. Librarians face the challenge of developing a collection that supports learning, teaching, and research needs, now and in the future, all with limited funds. DDA plans are intended to help address this challenge by being more responsive to immediate needs than traditional acquisition models.

Yet, librarians at Louisiana State University (LSU) Libraries recently ended all DDA plans in an attempt to more adequately meet user needs and support learning, teaching, and research. The focus of collection development shifted to large e-book collections. These met user preferences for titles without restrictions on printing and saving and provided simultaneous access for an unlimited number of users. Given these features, their potential for course use was examined. Through the subsequent process, course-adopted titles were identified and promoted as a library-funded alternative to the traditional student-purchased textbooks. This chapter details how the decision to terminate DDA plans and invest in e-book packages resulted in large upfront costs but enabled advantages in key areas of usability and curricular integration. Collecting and promoting high-quality course titles have allowed the libraries to drive e-book usage and engage in impactful collection development.

BACKGROUND

With ever-tightening financial constraints in recent years, the need for new, more efficient ways to purchase books became apparent. The enormous growth of e-book publications has allowed new business models to develop and has enabled purchasing at the point of need through DDA, as opposed to purchasing in advance of projected need via the approval plan model. DDA plans allow the library to build a profile of specific book collections based on factors like subject or cost and to load these MARC records into local catalog or discovery layers. Typically, there is no cost for patrons to view basic content, such as the table of contents, or during a brief preview period, usually less than ten minutes. If a title is used beyond this or if certain actions occur, such as a title download, the patron triggers a short-term loan (STL). This STL rents the books and charges the library a percentage of the retail cost of the title. A threshold number of STLs triggers the title to be purchased at the retail cost. The user experience with DDA offers seamless access to the title whether it is for a preview, STL, or full purchase. The application of a DDA plan offers immediate benefits. With minimal local resources in terms of staffing and time, the collection can be vastly increased. Librarians are able to engage users in the collection development process and purchase titles with immediate utility.

Nonetheless, DDA plans present limitations. Patrons have long influenced selection, and subject librarians work closely with faculty to receive input and recommendations. Under the DDA model, users' choices are harnessed and applied without a librarian serving as the intermediary, leaving librarians unsure of who exactly these selectors are. At LSU Libraries, given budget restrictions, understanding the profile of patron selectors was increasingly important as a way to determine if and to what degree new purchases supported the overall research needs of the campus. In addition to not clearly knowing who was making selection decisions, these patron selectors were working to fill short-term information needs, not strategizing to develop a long-lasting collection, leaving some librarians to question the long-term value of the investments.

DDA plans also pose usability challenges. The influx of records into the catalog provides the savvy researcher with a bounty of options from which to explore and select. But for other users, these additional titles can represent more noise in the search results, encouraging them to only select from the top results. In reflecting on DDA plans, Fister commented how "the recent Project Information Literacy Study clarifies something I've long sensed: undergraduates don't necessarily need a bigger banquet. They need a limited number of good choices, not all-you-can-eat."[1] Additionally, titles provided through DDA plans largely include digital rights management (DRM). DRM represents the technological restrictions applied to e-books and other digital media to prevent different types of unauthorized use. With e-books, these DRM restrictions are manifested through limitations on downloading and printing, requirement of additional accounts beyond the library account to access the title for checkout, and use of a proprietary e-book reader software.

Beginning in 2011, LSU Libraries explored this strategy with the vendor, Ebrary, focusing solely on e-books within the sciences. By repurposing and adapting an approval plan to the new e-DDA model, LSU Libraries was able to buy or "borrow" only books that were needed, when they were needed, without having to buy any that were not going to be used. This process was seen as a strategy to greatly reduce monographic expenditures while at the same time increase the number of titles available for immediate full-text access. Nearly a year and a half later the LSU Libraries decided to launch another DDA service using EBSCO as primary aggregator. The decision to add EBSCO occurred because the LSU Libraries had begun subscribing to the EBSCO e-book Academic Collection, and administratively it made more sense to consolidate and order through one vendor. After becoming more integrated into EBSCO's services, the Ebrary DDA plan was discontinued.

During that time, many of the public services staff anecdotally reported negative feedback from users regarding the e-book collection, including the vast number of titles added through DDA. Some of this was attributed to preference for print over electronic books, while others did not find the platforms user-friendly. Both factors can be seen in the literature on users' preferences and behaviors with e-books and e-textbooks. While some users state a preference for print books, Moore noted how libraries nonetheless see "usage statistics imply[ing] that e-books are being used at a much higher rate than their print counterparts."[2] Furthermore, research at the University of Ulster found that while users preferred print books, e-textbooks were the most popular type of e-book (56 percent of respondents) over other choices, including fiction, research monographs, and reference titles.[3] Moving beyond statements of preference, the majority of user complaints at LSU Libraries revolved around usability restrictions from DRM. Folb, Wessel, and Czechowski found that users value "printing, saving, and searching" features most with e-books—functions that are often restricted with DRM.[4] Similarly, Moore reviewed how users face a range of usability concerns when using e-books, including "difficulties with ease of use, general interface issues, problems with downloading to multiple devices and searching functionality, lack of Americans with Disabilities Act (ADA) compliance, the inability to annotate and highlight passages easily, too restrictive digital rights management (DRM)."[5]

At LSU Libraries, accessing e-book content through the larger DDA providers proved to be an onerous process. If users wanted to download material to their personal devices as opposed to reading the e-book in the native web-interface, several technical steps were required. Most titles required the additional software, Adobe Digital Editions, to be downloaded prior to download or checkout of the e-book material. Often patrons were required to log in to three different systems in order to access e-books. The first log-in was authenticating into the LSU Libraries, the second log-in had to be through the vendor's site, and the third log-in into Adobe Digital Editions. The issues experienced by users when interacting with titles from the DDA plans revealed major limitations. While the DDA plans allowed for a more expansive collection, most plans required DRM and represented a hoop that users were unhappy if not unwilling to jump through.

SHIFT AWAY FROM DDA

After over three years of using DDA through EBSCO and reflecting on its benefits and limitations, the decision was made to discontinue the process. This decision coincided with the arrival of a new dean in July 2014 and his application of a critical eye to established collection development practices. This triggered a shift away from the DDA model and was part of a sweeping collection development change that removed the majority of e-books with DRM from the collection. In their place, the libraries focused on investing in large e-book collections that met three essential criteria: DRM-free titles that allowed for an unlimited number of simultaneous users and provided perpetual access and archival rights. These principles were identified in the Charlotte Initiative for Permanent Acquisition of E-Books by Academic Libraries project funded by the Andrew W. Mellon Foundation's Scholarly Communications Program.[6]

Once the decision was made to only purchase e-book collections within this set of parameters and to forego purchases otherwise, LSU Libraries discontinued the DDA plan with EBSCO on July 15, 2014—two weeks into the new administration. All records were shadowed and removed. In their place, LSU Libraries purchased new and updated a significant number of e-book packages. These included De Gruyter Online University Press e-book Collections from Harvard University Press; Elsevier's Freedom Collection; GeoScienceWorld e-books; JSTOR e-books, UPCC Book Collections on Project Muse; Springer; and Wiley. Furthermore, titles available DRM-free for title-by-title purchasing were bought at the publisher level.

E-TEXTBOOK IMPACT OF THE SHIFT

A significant outcome of this change in policy has been how it enabled a textbook initiative. Traditionally, LSU Libraries did not intentionally collect textbooks despite a strong user demand from students for the library to provide alternatives to the traditional student-purchased model. Whereas previously the DRM and simultaneous user restrictions of e-books had prevented them from being used effectively as course materials, the focus on large e-books collections without DRM and the associated usability roadblocks positioned the library to respond to these user demands. This led to the recognition that the e-book collection could be aligned with required course textbooks to provide students with free access to required materials.

The libraries had been receiving a list of required textbooks from the campus bookstore in order to prevent students from interlibrary loaning course materials. Librarians informed the campus bookstore contact of the additional use to examine the bookstore list for matches with the e-book collection. This process initially occurred by visually reviewing the list for publishers included in the packages, but it became more automated by using scripts to scrape and match data. Regardless of the level of sophistication, the process allowed for the identification of course-adopted titles available within the e-book collections or for purchase title by title. Once identified and, if necessary, purchased, permalinks were shared with the affected faculty that could be embedded in the learning management system, course syllabus, or e-mailed to students. Additionally, a student-facing web page was created to promote all matching titles for each semester.

Quickly, this initiative proved to be a high-visibility avenue for connecting users with e-book collections. Since textbooks are materials critical for academic success, student and faculty feedback has been positive. Faculty appreciated how the use of a library-provided e-textbook meant that all students would have access to the title from the first day of class and would all be working with the same edition. Students appreciated e-book features like searchable text, the ability to save and print, and the portability of an e-book.

Beyond this, cost savings have represented the most important factor for students and a powerful way to convey impact to faculty and administrators. Exact cost savings have been difficult to pinpoint. First, the exact price students would have paid for the textbooks is not known. Students use a range of mechanisms to access textbooks: purchasing of new or used titles, renting or buying e-books, sharing copies with friends, photocopying or scanning a print copy, or pirating an illegal e-version. They can explore the cost of titles from different retail locations offering unique markups and discounts. As a result, a student can select among a variety of price points. Therefore, to calculate cost savings, librarians used the cost of a new print textbook from the campus bookstore. Second, pinpointing an actual enrollment number presents a challenge. Students drop a course after purchasing a textbook or add a class after the initial days of the semester. Some courses fail to meet full enrollment, but some exceed it and total seats are added to the course. Therefore, although imprecise, the librarians have used total potential enrollment—the course at full enrollment—captured at a point just prior to the start of the semester. This calculation makes assumptions, including that the course will be enrolled to capacity and that no students will purchase the textbook. In reality, courses fail to meet or exceed full enrollment and students use a variety of ways with a range of price points to access a textbook. Furthermore, while the goal of the program is to provide comprehensive access—something enabled with DRM-free titles—some students still choose to purchase a print copy due to preferences in reading format or a desire to build a personal library.

Once the number of students is multiplied by the textbook price, the potential cost savings for students is determined, as seen in figure 4.1. This number is gross and does not deduct the investments made by LSU Libraries

	FALL 2014	SPRING 2015	SUMMER 2015	FALL 2015	SPRING 2016
Textbooks	66	104	4	130	122
Classes	60	113	4	164	114
Students at full enrollment	2,270	2,379	150	6,399	4,546
Savings	$161,863	$288,412	$12,067	$476,263	$477,764

Figure 4.1 | **Potential E-Textbooks Savings by Semester**

to purchase these e-book collections. This information is then shared with a variety of stakeholders. It is broken down by academic colleges and shared with deans and is used in library annual report documents and promotional materials. The outcomes of the initiative were presented to the student government to raise awareness and encourage their promotion of the program.

Implications

The continual increase of textbook costs places a substantial burden on students, even more so for those needing financial assistance (defined as grants, scholarships, or loans) where on average "70% of their total textbook expenses [are] covered by financial aid."[7] According to the College Board's Annual Survey of Colleges, 2015–16, the average cost of textbooks nears $1,300 per student per year for a public four-year institution.[8] To further illustrate the strain that students feel, a 2013 Government Accountability Office report on college textbooks found that between 2002 and 2012 textbook prices rose 82 percent.[9] This helps to explain why it is difficult for students to find cost-saving options when new textbook prices rise at a cost increase four times the rate of inflation.[10]

In addition, a 2013 Student Public Interest Research Group study indicated that "65% of students said they had decided against buying a textbook because it was too expensive," and also noted that "students are not only choosing not to purchase the materials they are assigned by their professor, but they are knowingly accepting the risk of a lower grade to avoid paying for the textbook."[11] Additional studies by the Florida Virtual Campus and Nebraska Book Company as referenced by Gallant indicate that "the cost of textbooks caused thirty-one percent of [students] to decline registering for a course" and "nearly half of students surveyed would choose one university over another if they offered free textbooks for all four years of undergraduate college."[12]

Concerns related to the cost of textbooks are almost universally felt by students at LSU, and strategies to reduce the escalating cost of higher education have become a focal point in the state. This collection development strategy acts as a tool to mitigate the cost of higher education. Purchasing e-book collections that enable use of the titles in classes and promoting their role as such have driven usage and positioned the libraries in a relevant role (see figure 4.2).

This process began with the decision to terminate DDA plans and the concerted effort to add many new titles to the collection. By prioritizing titles without DRM, these e-books provided a user-friendly experience. Through strong promotion to ensure awareness, these new large packages received impressive use, as demonstrated in figure 4.3. Usage metrics reflected in COUNTER Book Reports 2 showed a 40 percent increase of chapter downloads and usage from fiscal year 2014 to fiscal year 2015, which is the time frame when DDA was canceled. Within that one year, approximately 17,000 unique e-book titles were used by our students, faculty, and staff.

Upon implementation of the e-textbook initiative, increase in the usage of e-book titles used as course materials was almost immediate. As an example, one title used in a fall 2014 course continued to have consistent and extensive

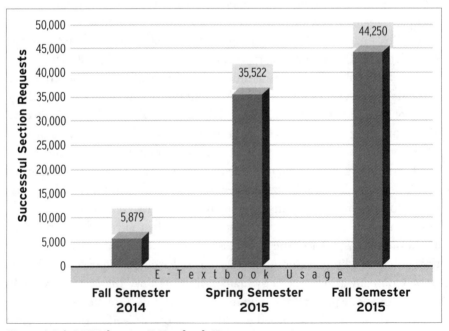

Figure 4.2 | **LSU Libraries E-Textbook Usage**

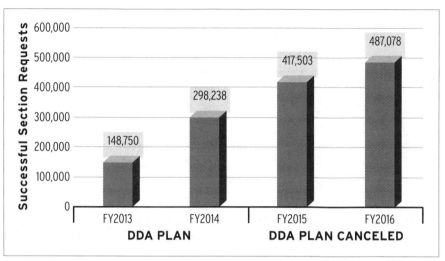

Figure 4.3 | **LSU Libraries E-Book Usage**

usage the following spring when the specific course was not offered. This particular title, which is part of the engineering curriculum, now averages 20,000 chapter downloads a year. This high and steady usage anecdotally suggests a word-of-mouth marketing campaign among students in need of curriculum support regardless of course enrollment status.

CONCLUSION

The LSU Libraries views the addition of e-books that can be used as course materials as a critical component to the collection. This is a new step and a shift away from a legacy practice that deemed textbooks as unacceptable expenditures. By tailoring and customizing e-book acquisitions to fit user needs (DRM-free, perpetual access, unlimited simultaneous users), the Libraries was able to provide financial relief to students and continued robust support of university teaching and learning. Alignment with courses drove use and provided a compelling use case for librarians eager to highlight to administrators the importance and value of investment in e-book collections. This initiative can continue to be built through future large package and title-by-title purchases of e-books with the usability principles that enable use in the classroom and can be expanded by exploring additional cost-saving measures for students such as open-access solutions and open educational resources.

Notes

1. Barbara Fister, "Puzzled by Patron-Driven Acquisitions," *Inside Higher Ed* (blog), November 11, 2010, https://www.insidehighered.com/blogs/library_babel_fish/puzzled_by_patron_driven_acquisitions.
2. Kate Moore, "Are We There Yet? Moving to an E-Only Collection Development Policy for Books," *Serials Librarian* 68, no. 1–4 (2015): 127–36, doi: 10.1080/0361526X.2015.1016836.
3. Sarah Smyth and Andrew P. Carlin, "Use and Perception of E-Books in the University of Ulster: A Case Study," *New Review of Academic Librarianship* 18, no. 2 (2012): 176–205, doi:10.1080/13614533.2012.719851.
4. Barbara Folb, Charles B. Wessel, and Leslie J. Czechowski, "Clinical and Academic Use of Electronic and Print Books: The Health Sciences Library System E-Book Study at the University of Pittsburgh," *Journal of the Medical Library Association* 99, no. 3 (2011): 218–28, doi: 10.3163/1536–5050.99.3.009.
5. Moore, "Are We There Yet?" 131.
6. "Charlotte Initiative," UNC Charlotte, last modified June 13, 2016, http://guides.library.uncc.edu/Charlotteinitiative.
7. Student Public Interest Research Groups, 2016, "Covering the Cost," Student PIRGs, www.studentpirgs.org/textbooks.
8. The College Board, 2016, "Average Estimated Undergraduate Budgets, 2015–16," Collegeboard.org, https://trends.collegeboard.org/college-pricing/figures-tables/average-estimated-undergraduate-budgets-2015–16.
9. United States Government Accountability Office, 2013, "College Textbooks: Students Have Greater Access to Textbook Information," Report to Congressional Committees, June, GAO-13–368, www.gao.gov/assets/660/655066.pdf.
10. Student Public Interest Research Groups, 2016, "Covering the Cost," Student PIRGs, www.studentpirgs.org/textbooks.
11. Student Public Interest Research Groups, 2014, "Fixing the Broken Textbook Market: How Students Respond to Higher Textbook Costs and Demand Alternatives," Student PIRGs, www.studentpirgs.org/textbooks.
12. Jeff Gallant, "Librarians Transforming Textbooks: The Past, Present, and Future of the Affordable Learning Georgia Initiative," *Georgia Library Quarterly* 52, no. 2 (2015): 12–17.

Bibliography

"Charlotte Initiative." UNC Charlotte, last modified June 13, 2016. http://guides.library.uncc.edu/Charlotteinitiative.

College Board. 2016. "Average Estimated Undergraduate Budgets, 2015–16." Collegeboard .org. https://trends.collegeboard.org/college-pricing/figures-tables/average-estimated -undergraduate-budgets-2015–16.

Fister, Barbara. "Puzzled by Patron-Driven Acquisitions." *Inside Higher Ed* (blog). November 11, 2010. https://www.insidehighered.com/blogs/library_babel_fish/puzzled_by _patron_driven_acquisitions.

Folb, Barbara, Charles B. Wessel, and Leslie J. Czechowski. "Clinical and Academic Use of Electronic and Print Books: The Health Sciences Library System E-Book Study at the University of Pittsburgh." *Journal of the Medical Library Association* 99, no. 3 (2011): 218–28. doi: 10.3163/1536–5050.99.3.009.

Gallant, Jeff. "Librarians Transforming Textbooks: The Past, Present, and Future of the Affordable Learning Georgia Initiative." *Georgia Library Quarterly* 52, no. 2 (2015): 12–17.

Moore, Katie. "Are We There Yet? Moving to an E-Only Collection Development Policy for Books." *Serials Librarian* 68, no. 1–4 (2015): 127–36. doi: 10.1080/0361526X.2015 .1016836.

Smyth, Sarah, and Andrew P. Carlin. "Use and Perception of E-Books in the University of Ulster: A Case Study." *New Review of Academic Librarianship* 18, no. 2 (2012): 176–205. doi:10.1080/13614533.2012.719851.

Student Public Interest Research Groups. 2014. "Fixing the Broken Textbook Market: How Students Respond to Higher Textbook Costs and Demand Alternatives." Student PIRGs. www.studentpirgs.org/textbooks.

———. 2016. "Covering the Cost." Student PIRGs. www.studentpirgs.org/textbooks.

United States Government Accountability Office. June 2013. "College Textbooks: Students Have Greater Access to Textbook Information." Report to Congressional Committees, GAO-13–368. www.gao.gov/assets/660/655066.pdf.

TEXTBOOKS AND COURSE ADOPTION MATERIALS AT NEW YORK UNIVERSITY SHANGHAI

Michael Hughes

New York University Shanghai is the newest degree-granting campus in NYU's global network. After opening in August 2013, on the campus of East China Normal University (ECNU) in the Putuo District of Shanghai, China, the campus moved to its current permanent location in a newly constructed building in the Pudong District in August 2014. The campus opened with a class of 300 undergraduates and fewer than 40 faculty members in the first year, and the library now supports the undergraduate learning of 900 students (expected to grow to a maximum of 2,000), as well as teaching and research across the liberal arts, with considerable focus on business and STEM (science, technology, engineering, and mathematics), and a faculty that has more than doubled.[1] The language of instruction, and the primary language of the collection, is English. Given the location of the campus, procurement of student textbooks is a more involved process than it would be for an institution in the United States. From the beginning, the library has played a central role in providing course materials for the students at NYU Shanghai, and has developed a comprehensive approach to textbooks and other course materials. Currently, this approach has two components, which were developed sequentially. The first component involves collecting all textbooks and course materials required for any class taught on the Shanghai campus, and ensuring that those materials are made available on course reserve; the second involves providing or identifying electronic versions of course materials and, where possible, purchasing a multiuser license for use of those materials by classes in lieu of print textbooks. This chapter will discuss how the approach was developed, outline the policies and procedures currently in place for textbooks and course adoption materials in the library, and discuss outcomes. At the end, brief discussion will be made of a third phase, currently in the planning stages.

BACKGROUND

The year prior to opening the library on the ECNU campus was spent planning and laying the groundwork for the resources and services that would be available to the incoming faculty and students in fall 2013. Since the library of NYU Shanghai is administratively part of the NYU Division of Libraries, it has been developed with substantial support from staff, administrators, and librarians in New York. In the initial planning stages, in fact, all of the work was done by the New York staff and librarians, as there was no Shanghai-based staff until June 2013, when the access services librarian arrived. On the collections side of the operation, multiple meetings were held, both in person and virtually, involving representatives from both the library (including the collection development librarian, the dean of libraries, and the associate deans of collections and public services) and the academic leadership of NYU Shanghai (including the vice chancellor, the provost, the dean of arts and sciences, and the dean of academic affairs). In addition to discussions of the curriculum and the general outlines of the collection to be built over the first few years, plans were made for how to support courses more directly. Very early on it was decided that the library collection at NYU Shanghai would deviate from the common policy at NYU of excluding textbooks; in fact, the acquisition of textbooks and course adoption materials used in the classes at NYU Shanghai would not only be encouraged, but would be an essential part of the early steps in building the collection.

A few considerations went into this decision. There are many ways in which NYU Shanghai is different from the other NYU global campuses, but most relevant to the current discussion is the way textbooks are ordered and distributed. At both the New York and Abu Dhabi campuses, textbooks are ordered and sold by the university bookstore; but NYU Shanghai has no bookstore. This is something that came up during the planning meetings, which allowed us to prepare for the difficulties that could arise. Without a bookstore, it is the Academic Affairs staff, working with the staff in the Procurement office, who order textbooks for the students, alongside their other duties. The textbooks are then distributed to the students at the start of classes, rather than purchased individually at a university bookstore. Further, since the language of instruction is English, all of the textbooks must be ordered from the United States through companies approved by the Chinese government, adding layers of complexity to the ordering and shipping processes. We anticipated that there could be considerable delays in the delivery of books using this method, on top of expected delivery times of 6–8 weeks for most books, with some as long as 8–11 weeks. It was clear early on that the library could take steps to minimize the distraction to students and faculty caused by late-arriving textbooks.

PRINT COURSE MATERIALS

Since the library at NYU Shanghai is part of the NYU Division of Libraries, we were well-positioned to ameliorate some of the anticipated difficulties before they arose. The acquisition and processing of materials for NYU Shanghai are done in or through New York, taking advantage of many of the workflows already established for our New York collections. Likewise, the development of the NYU Shanghai library benefited from lessons learned in opening NYU Abu Dhabi in fall 2010. The collection development librarian and the technical services staff for NYU Shanghai are based in New York, which fosters close integration with the Division of Libraries as a whole. In addition to increasing the efficiency with which titles are ordered and processed, this allows us to ship our materials to Shanghai using a different method from what would be necessary if the orders were placed in China, as is the case for student copies of textbooks.

The long duration and expected delays in shipping of student textbooks, coupled with an attempt to account for unforeseen problems bound to occur when opening a new campus, were the main forces driving our decision to ensure that course materials would be available in the library. However, there was another potential issue taken into consideration in our approach to textbooks:

the possibility that some books might be stopped at customs for political reasons. NYU Shanghai was founded on the condition that NYU would operate according to the principles of academic freedom, and the library collection is developed to support the needs of teaching and research at NYU Shanghai in accord with both the ALA Library Bill of Rights (American Library Association 2006a) and the Intellectual Freedom Principles for Academic Libraries (American Library Association 2006b). At the time of this writing, no library materials have been refused or confiscated by customs officials, nor do we anticipate that happening. However, there remain regulations governing the Chinese companies tasked with importing student textbooks into China; and in the initial planning stages, it was anticipated that there might be delays or refusals of certain course adoption books, preventing them from arriving for the students, either on time or at all.[2] In at least one case, the library was able to provide unlimited electronic access (in addition to a print copy in the collection) to a book the vendors supplying student textbooks were unable to import to China, for whatever reason.

With these considerations in mind, it was decided that we would collect all textbooks and course adoption books mentioned on any syllabus, whether listed under required or recommended reading, and do so using the general collections budget. Furthermore, all books for courses would initially be added to course reserves without requiring a request from the instructor. We reasoned that, on top of the usual hectic pace of preparing courses for the semester, the fact that NYU Shanghai was a new endeavor would simply add to the difficulties faced by instructors as they prepared their classes; since we could easily alleviate the burden of this one task with books we were already ordering, we did so. In the case of print books, a copy was placed on reserve; for e-books, authenticating links were created for the course page in the course management system. Once the first semester had started, the access services librarian reached out to the faculty to let them know that their materials had been placed on reserve. Needless to say, the response from the faculty was very positive.

This last point highlights a major component in the development of the library in general, and of the collection and course support in particular: early and consistent communication with the faculty about library resources and services. Since the library opened with minimal staff, certain responsibilities that would usually fall to access services were taken on by the collection development librarian, including much of the early communication about textbooks and course materials. This was a natural fit, because the collection development librarian was already reaching out to faculty regarding their collection needs during the spring and summer of 2013. The communication began with an e-mail sent to each incoming faculty member introducing the collection development librarian and the library in general.[3] The response rate for the first e-mails sent was 87 percent. While not every instructor requested assistance, all who responded were very interested to learn about the library resources and services, and this presented an early opportunity to communicate directly with faculty members. This early outreach helped to develop a strong relationship between the faculty and the library that has been beneficial in many ways.

On a procedural level, in order to fulfill these new collection requirements, it was necessary to have copies of each syllabus early enough in the process to ensure that library copies of the course books could be ordered and delivered in time for the semester. Despite the relationships being developed with individual faculty members, it was decided that the library would not ask them directly for their syllabi. Rather, during the spring of 2013, the collection development librarian reached out to staff in the Academic Affairs office, requesting syllabi and textbook lists, while at the same time offering library collections and services to help the staff perform their duties, such as the compilation of course packs. Whereas the staff had previously been responsible for finding materials for course packs themselves, they could now work with the library to acquire these materials.[4] This mutual assistance helped to develop a close working relationship between the library and the Academic Affairs office that has proved invaluable. As it turned out, there were several books in the fall semester of 2013 that did not arrive in Shanghai until several weeks into the semester. Some of these delays were due to unforeseen shipping delays, while others were the result of late requests by faculty, or even just the difficulties inherent in opening a new campus. As a result of the cooperation established between the library and the Academic Affairs office, the library copies were available, and the faculty were able to take advantage of their assigned materials without delay.

The practice of early sharing of syllabi and early ordering of both required and recommended readings for the library collection continues each semester. There is now a full library staff to support courses through print reserves. There are also multiple lines of communication among the staff, librarians, faculty, and administration, allowing this process to continue fairly routinely. Given the increase in the number of students and classes, the breadth of the automatic addition of titles to print reserves has been reduced recently. Only required readings are now placed on reserve automatically; recommended and optional readings are placed on reserve at the faculty member's request. By default, a single copy of each required book is placed on reserve; at the instructor's request, one additional copy per fifteen students enrolled can be added. In addition to readings, films and videos in DVD or Blu-ray format are also supplied for courses. Course packs are not placed on reserve, but are provided to the students along with their textbooks by the Academic Affairs office.

ELECTRONIC COURSE MATERIALS

As with the development of the collection, Internet access at NYU Shanghai is provided in accordance with the Intellectual Freedom Principles (American Library Association 2006b) and is not limited by the so-called Great Firewall, a government-sponsored Internet censorship program in China. Furthermore, when possible any electronic resource licensed to NYU is licensed for global use by members of the entire NYU community, Shanghai and Abu Dhabi inclusive. It was always intended that the rich electronic resources of NYU would play a large role in the collection at NYU Shanghai. Thus, in addition to the print books acquired for course reserve discussed above, the library has from the beginning offered a service providing links to library-licensed resources for instructors and students, almost exclusively in the form of journal articles, but also including e-book chapters. Building on this as early as September 2013, the collection development librarian encouraged the use of licensed library resources (and specifically e-books) in place of print textbooks where possible, meeting with the dean of academic affairs to discuss this. While nothing formal was instituted at that time, over the next two semesters informal efforts were made to substitute print books by their electronic counterparts in a handful of cases. Although the faculty in general were understanding of the difficulties and expense involved in ordering individual student copies of print textbooks, many of them were uncomfortable with replacing print copies by e-books. Anecdotal concerns included the oft-expressed issues of dislike for reading on a screen for an extended period of time, to other less commonly voiced concerns such as the divergent page layout and unclear pagination in, for example, Oxford Scholarship Online titles, or the awkwardness of consulting endnotes when using e-books.[5]

In the fall of 2014, after NYU Shanghai moved to its new building, the director of the library began working with the dean of academic affairs on a project to study the possibility of replacing student copies of textbooks with library copies at a ratio of one copy for every fifteen students. When possible, the library copy would be electronic, but the option of providing multiple library copies of print books on reserve was also studied. In order to determine what impact this would have on textbook ordering, a retrospective study was done on the final textbook list of the fall semester 2014 (i.e., books already ordered and received). In addition to calculating the potential cost of multiple library copies of print books based on the 1:15 copy-to-student ratio, there were two categories of e-books considered: library-licensed e-books, and e-books available on another platform to be purchased or rented for the students. The former would be purchased using the library general collection budget, while the latter would be paid for by the students with their tuition, in the same way personal copies of print textbooks are financed at NYU Shanghai. The main criterion for library e-books was that the copy had to be licensed for unlimited simultaneous use, but it was not required that the copy be DRM-free. For the personal e-books to be rented or purchased on behalf of each student, the preferred platform was the Amazon Kindle due to the wide range of hardware devices covered,[6] but other platforms were also included in the study. If an e-book of the title was available through the library (held or available for purchase by the library) then there was no further searching; only if the library would have been unable to provide an e-book was the search extended to include individual copies for the students. Of the textbooks ordered for the fall 2014 semester, 9 of 105 titles (roughly 8.5 percent) could have been replaced with qualifying library-licensed e-books, while 50 (roughly 48 percent) were available on the Kindle, and 12 (roughly 11 percent) more were available through the publisher's website. Seeing that roughly 67 percent of the print textbooks could have been provided electronically, it was decided to undertake a pilot project for the spring semester.[7]

In order to do this, it was necessary to bring together the three departments that would be involved (the library, Academic Technology Services, and Academic Affairs) to develop policies and workflows. The library was represented by the collection development librarian and the access services librarian along with staff from Academic Technology Services (ATS) (part of the library), who met with representatives of the Academic Affairs office to establish the procedures. Since the Academic Affairs office compiles the initial list of required textbooks, it was agreed that the list would be shared as a Google spreadsheet (NYU uses Google Apps for Education). The list would first be reviewed by the library, followed by ATS, ultimately returning to the Academic Affairs staff. The Academic Affairs staff selected courses for the pilot, compiled the list, and shared the sheet. The process developed in that meeting, described immediately below, was adopted and continues to be used.

At each stage in the process, the shared spreadsheet is updated. When there is a library copy, an authenticating link to the e-book is copied into the appropriate cell so everyone knows not only that there is a copy, but how to access it.[8] If there is no library e-book available, that is indicated in the appropriate cell. If there is no library e-book available, and the library does not yet hold a print copy of the title, then a print copy is ordered for the collection and placed on reserve for the course. Once the library has reviewed the list, it is taken up by ATS. The next step is for ATS staff to search for Kindle books to fulfill the remaining orders if possible. When a Kindle book is identified, the appropriate cell is filled in with cost information as well as the book's ASIN or a link to the Amazon.com page. Once course registration is complete, the Academic Affairs office shares the course roster with ATS. ATS staff then purchase copies of the Kindle book with funds provided by the Academic Affairs office, and distribute them to the students using Amazon's Whispercast platform. Finally, if no electronic version is available, the Academic Affairs office works with the Procurement office to import personal copies for the students.

Based on feedback from the dean of academic affairs, the pilot was successful, and it was decided that this procedure would be implemented each semester for all classes beginning in fall 2015. The success of this project rested on preexisting procedures and relationships we had developed over the previous year in implementing our print reserves: syllabus sharing, help securing texts for course packs, providing a linking service, and so on. Additionally, the strong relationships the library and other involved departments had begun to develop with the faculty helped to ensure that the switch to electronic textbooks was not seen as simply an imposition from the administration. The percentage of titles we have been able to provide electronically has increased slightly since the initial study. Most recently, for the fall semester 2016, the library was able to provide 29 of 179 titles as library-licensed e-books (16 percent) while an additional 105 titles were identified as being available for purchase or rental in individual electronic format (59 percent), for a total of 75 percent of textbook titles (an increase of 8 percent from the initial study).

CONCLUSION AND NEXT STEPS

In the face of unique challenges associated with opening a university in China, the library at NYU Shanghai has taken a proactive role in ensuring that course materials are available to the students and faculty. From the early decision to collect all textbooks, and continuing through the development and implementation of a procedure for fulfilling textbook needs electronically, the key to success has been continuous and active communication among the library, the faculty, and the administration. This cooperation has led to a significant reduction in the overhead of providing textbooks, as well as fostering a spirit of collaboration between the library and the faculty. The librarians at NYU Shanghai continue to look for opportunities to improve support for the students and faculty there. Building on the initiatives described in this chapter, the collection development librarian and the library director are developing a pilot project of library support for the selection and adoption of open educational resources at NYU Shanghai, which could further alleviate many of the difficulties and complications inherent in providing print textbooks, not least of which is the high price of textbooks, both print and electronic, for the students. In the initial phase, one or two faculty members will be approached and asked to consider adopting an open textbook for the spring semester of 2017, with expansion expected in subsequent semesters. Given the excellent communication established between the faculty and the library, particularly around the topic of textbooks and course materials, there is good reason to be optimistic that this new project will be a success.

Notes

1. For a discussion of the challenges involved in opening and running American-style academic libraries around the world, see Pun, Collard, and Parrott 2016, including a chapter on collection development in Shanghai and NYU Abu Dhabi by the author (DeDonato and Hughes 2016).

2. To understand the context for these concerns, see, for example, Buckley 2015 for a discussion of recent statements by a government official on the use and importation of "Western" textbooks in China. NYU Shanghai was not among the universities addressed by the official. For a more in-depth discussion of these concerns, along with testimony of representatives of Sino-American universities in China, including NYU Shanghai, see the transcript and other documents from the House Subcommittee on Africa, Global Health, Global Human Rights, and International Organizations hearing, "Is Academic Freedom Threatened by China's Influence on U.S. Universities?" (House of Representatives 2015).

3. The main text of that initial e-mail reads: "I am the Librarian for Shanghai Collections, working in New York. I'm writing to introduce myself, and to let you know that I am available to answer any library collections questions you might have. If you are planning to be in New York this summer, I would love to meet with you to discuss how the

Shanghai library collection can support your needs. I will also be in contact with you in the next couple of days regarding your list of books you'd like us to purchase. If I can be of any help to you, please do not hesitate to contact me."

4. Prior to the founding of NYU Shanghai, there was an NYU study away program in place at ECNU. Many of the staff making up the Academic Affairs office in the early days had previously worked for the study away program. Likewise, a handful of NYU Shanghai instructors had taught in the program.

5. Many of the objections voiced were the same as those commonly seen in the literature. See, for example, the reviews by Slater (Slater 2010) and Staiger (Staiger 2012) for extended discussions of common obstacles to the widespread acceptance of e-books in academic libraries.

6. Since books available for the Amazon Kindle can be read on PCs, Macs, tablets, and phones in addition to Kindle devices, there was no need to purchase new hardware for each student to use these books.

7. This project was not initially undertaken to reduce materials costs for the institution, but to alleviate difficulties with shipping. The only significant savings in material costs come when the library is able to provide an e-book; individual-use e-books have not been shown to lead to a significant cost reduction. Based on the study of textbooks ordered in fall 2014, the savings in materials would have been less than $10,000 had copies of every available e-book been ordered that semester, and the print counterparts not ordered. That comes out to less than 5 percent of the actual textbook costs incurred that semester. However, there are significant savings for the Academic Affairs office in shipping and ordering costs when using this method.

8. If the library does not yet have access to a qualifying e-book, a copy is ordered and the authenticating link is added to the spreadsheet when it is available.

Bibliography

American Library Association. 2006a. "Library Bill of Rights." Advocacy, Legislation & Issues. June 30. www.ala.org/advocacy/intfreedom/librarybill/.

———. 2006b. "Intellectual Freedom Principles for Academic Libraries." Advocacy, Legislation & Issues. July 26. www.ala.org/advocacy/intfreedom/librarybill/interpretations/intellectual.

Buckley, Chris. 2015. "China Warns Against 'Western Values' in Imported Textbooks." *Sinosphere Blog.* January 30. http://sinosphere.blogs.nytimes.com/2015/01/30/china-warns-against-western-values-in-imported-textbooks/.

DeDonato, Ree, and Michael Hughes. 2016. "Collection Development for Global Campus Libraries." In *Bridging Worlds : Emerging Models and Practices of U.S. Academic Libraries around the Globe,* 81–90. Chicago: Association of College and Research Libraries, a division of the American Library Association.

House of Representatives. 2015. "Is Academic Freedom Threatened by China's Influence on U.S. Universities?: Hearing before the Subcommittee on Africa, Global Health, Global Human Rights, and International Organizations of the Committee on Foreign Affairs." 114th Cong. https://foreignaffairs.house.gov/hearing/subcommittee-hearingis-academic -freedom-threatened-by-chinas-influence-on-u-s-universities-2/.

Pun, Raymond, Scott Collard, and Justin Parrott, eds. 2016. *Bridging Worlds: Emerging Models and Practices of U.S. Academic Libraries around the Globe.* Chicago: Association of College and Research Libraries, a division of the American Library Association.

Slater, Robert. 2010. "Why Aren't E-Books Gaining More Ground in Academic Libraries? E-Book Use and Perceptions: A Review of Published Literature and Research." *Journal of Web Librarianship* 4, no. 4: 305–31. doi: 10.1080/19322909.2010.525419.

Staiger, Jeff. 2012. "How E-Books Are Used: A Literature Review of the E-Book Studies Conducted from 2006 to 2011." *Reference & User Services Quarterly* 51, no. 4: 355–65.

6

THE NORTH CAROLINA STATE UNIVERSITY LIBRARIES' ALT-TEXTBOOK PROJECT

Open Education That Opens a Door to the Library

Kristine Alpi, William Cross, Greg Raschke, and Madison Sullivan

This chapter introduces the North Carolina State University (NCSU) Libraries' Alt-Textbook Project, a library-driven program designed to encourage NCSU faculty to consider open educational resources and other alternatives to expensive commercial textbooks. This chapter situates the Alt-Textbook project in the context of the larger open education movement as well as within library efforts to reduce textbook costs and enhance equitable access to diverse learning materials. It also describes how the project connects the libraries with campus stakeholders, demonstrates the value of library collections, services, and expertise, and sparks discussion about textbook affordability and open culture across the university.

BACKGROUND

The increase of textbook costs combined with the continual evolution of technologies that deliver course content has made the "textbook problem" ripe for systemic change. While course materials are a vital part of the higher education system, cost increases well above the general rate of inflation have exacerbated dissatisfaction with standard textbook publishing and delivery models.[1] Though students can spend less than the College Board reports through e-books and rentals, the escalation of textbook prices well above the overall rate of inflation continues unabated. The Government Accountability Office estimates that from 2002 to 2013 prices increased by 82 percent, three times the rate of increase in overall consumer prices.[2] This rate of increase is driven by a variety of factors, but at its core it stems from a generally inelastic market where consumers (students) and providers (publisher/vendor/bookstore) are separated by an intermediary (instructor) who is not directly exposed to price unless the instructor is the author of the text. Though inelastic in structure, the significant rate of increase in costs has helped increase awareness and dissatisfaction among participants in the textbook market. From this crossroads of unsustainable costs, emerging delivery technologies, and growing dissatisfaction, the long-term evolution of systems for delivering course materials will be shaped by a complex mix of economic, political, pedagogical, and technological factors. This evolution will also be shaped by a diverse set of players that includes students, faculty, publishers, open educational resource providers, information technologists, and librarians.

The immediate problem facing academic libraries is what, if anything, we can or should do about the textbook problem. Even though libraries have a long record of providing access to course materials through reserve systems, both print and online, libraries, particularly in North America, have traditionally taken a hands-off approach to the textbook problem. No library has the funding or mandate to purchase textbooks at the scale needed to serve an entire institution of students. Since they neither select nor use textbooks, libraries have not been principal agents of change in the textbook market. That traditional stance on textbooks, however, is rapidly changing—and for good reason.

At the NCSU Libraries, our efforts to more directly address the textbook problem on behalf of students and faculty began with a resolution from students asking us to place one copy of every required textbook on print reserve. This commitment has evolved into a multimodal effort to provide short-term assistance to students while pursuing long-term systemic change in the market and within our university. The NCSU Libraries pursue a number of approaches to aid students and instructors in dealing with the various challenges associated with textbooks, including:

1. in partnership with the NCSU bookstores, purchasing at least one copy of every required textbook and offering them through print reserves;[3]

2. purchasing a site license in 2010 for *Physics Curriculum & Instruction,* an experimental physics textbook used by 1,300 NCSU students who take introductory physics courses each semester. This was provided as a free e-textbook or inexpensive print-on-demand textbook in 2010 for use in introductory courses, hosting its availability for all authorized NCSU users, and providing a print-on-demand option through the bookstores;[4]

3. developing a suite of advocacy materials about the textbook problem and potential market-moving solutions such as OERs; and

4. building on the excellent leadership of projects in the libraries at Temple University and the University of Massachusetts-Amherst which offer mini-grants to faculty members who adopt or create OERs to replace expensive assigned textbooks to develop an alternative textbook program.[5]

As hubs that connect stakeholders across higher education institutions, libraries have a natural connection to students and their growing dissatisfaction with textbook costs. Libraries also work closely with faculty across the life cycle of their research and teaching. Library service provision and engagement with pedagogical utilities such as electronic reserves and course management systems increased engagement with digital tools for delivering course materials. More libraries are leveraging the combination of student dissatisfaction, faculty interest in new teaching and learning approaches, established relationships with both students and faculty, and the burgeoning OER offerings to engage in the textbook conversation and offer solutions. OERs and alternative market-driven options such as Flat World Knowledge and OpenStax have created opportunities for libraries to come off the sidelines of the textbook problem and start participating in the development, promotion, and dissemination of alternatives.

While academic libraries do not exert central authority or market power to drive solutions, they do have both physical centrality on campuses and important visibility and goodwill. Furthermore, strategies are available for librarians to move the needle on problems of affordability and access by piloting new approaches to incubate change. The rising number of incentive and grant programs for incubating alternatives to traditional textbooks points to libraries as engines that drive change by providing educational resource solutions to their students and faculty that enable both cost savings and innovative approaches to teaching and learning.[6] At the NCSU Libraries, we aimed to create a program that promoted both effective learning and cost-effectiveness by leveraging and highlighting library expertise.

THE NCSU LIBRARIES' ALT-TEXTBOOK PROJECT

"Free and Better": Developing the Alt-Textbook Project

Recognizing the financial pressures facing our students and the opportunity for the libraries to address them through collaborating with faculty to seed innovation, in 2013 the NCSU Libraries began developing our Alt-Textbook program. We took inspiration from alt-textbook programs hosted at the Temple University Libraries and University of Massachusetts at Amherst Libraries. Like these programs, NCSU's Alt-Textbook project provides small grants of between $500 and $2,000 to individual instructors who are willing to replace an existing commercial textbook with an open educational resource.

In order to develop the project, we needed to locate two resources: model documents to guide our development of content for publicizing, managing, and awarding the grants, and the actual funds to be provided for awards. For the model documents, we looked to Temple and UMass-Amherst. Fortunately, those libraries welcomed us to the OER community and offered a host of useful resources and insights. For funding, we explored several options, including grants. A $15,000 award from the North Carolina State University Foundation provided the financial resources for a pilot program. Figure 6.1 is a press release announcing the grant, figure 6.2 is a call for proposals, and figure 6.3 is our rubric for evaluating proposals.

NCSU News Release

NCSU Libraries offering grants to help faculty develop free or low-cost open textbook alternatives

Media Contact: David Hiscoe, 919-513-3425

Date: August xx, 2014

FOR IMMEDIATE RELEASE

(Raleigh, N.C.)—In the latest of several initiatives designed to help students reduce the expense of textbooks as part of their university educations and make it easier for faculty to explore and create new resources for their teaching, the NCSU Libraries is inviting North Carolina State University faculty to apply for grants to adopt, adapt, or create free or low-cost open alternatives to today's expensive textbooks.

Ranging between $500 and $2,000, the competitive *Alt-Textbook* grants will be awarded to help faculty pursue innovative uses of technology and information resources that can replace pricey traditional textbooks. Larger grants may be available for larger-scale or especially high-impact projects.

Textbook costs have outpaced inflation by 300% over the last 30 years. These runaway prices have become a major strain on students, with textbooks averaging $1,200 a year and 7 out of 10 students admitting on a recent Public Interest Research Group survey that they have not purchased a required text because of its cost.

Grants are available to develop textbook alternatives for the Spring 2015 and Fall 2015 semesters. Possible approaches include:

- creating a new open textbook or collection of materials
- adopting an existing open textbook
- assembling a collection of open resources into new course materials
- licensing an e-textbook, video, or other media content for classroom use or e-reserves
- using subscribed library resources

As faculty work on their proposals, NCSU librarians are available to collaborate and to share expertise in copyright, licensing, open access, course management software and tools, electronic reserves, subject-matter content, and multimedia resources.

"Academic libraries have always been a powerful way to reduce the financial burden of a university education by pooling key resources for everyone to use," reminds Susan K. Nutter, Vice Provost and Director of the NCSU Libraries. "The *Alt-Textbook* grants offer an innovative way to leverage that advantage in the digital age while at the same time giving our faculty a powerful tool to tailor their course materials to the exact needs of their students."

The NCSU Libraries will hold several information sessions about the project in September. Faculty can learn more about the project, review the call for proposals, sign up for information sessions, and download grant applications at the *Alt-Textbook* Project website.

The *Alt-Textbook* initiative builds on a successful partnership with the university's Physics Department that resulted in a free physics e-textbook that is now used by 1,300 NC State students each year.

Other NCSU Libraries initiatives to reduce costs for students include providing at least one copy of every required course book on reserve each semester, supplying online reserves to electronically disseminate materials within the bounds of copyright law, and Library Course Tools, an innovative use of the Libraries' website to present custom, course-related library content for every course at the university.

Alt-Textbook is supported by a grant from the NC State University Foundation.

Figure 6.1 | **Alt-Textbook Grants Press Release**

[Subject Line]
NCSU Libraries grants available for innovative open learning materials

[Body]
Interested in grant funding to explore new resources for your teaching? Excited about innovative educational resources like video and open/online materials? Want to reduce your students' debt load? The NCSU Libraries invites applications for a competitive grant program to adopt, adapt, or create free or low-cost alternatives to expensive textbooks.

Open Educational Resources (OERs) are freely accessible alternatives to traditional print textbooks. OERs empower faculty to innovate pedagogically, enhance access for NC State students to high-quality, tailored educational materials, and reduce the financial burden of expensive textbooks. The NCSU Libraries' Alt-Textbook program wants to fund your ideas for an OER or other textbook alternative in your class. Whether you're interested in opening up an existing textbook like the Libraries and Physics Department did for Physics 211 and 212 or designing a next-generation package of online resources and videos, the Alt-Textbook Project can fund your great idea with a grant of between **$500** and **$2,000** (larger grants may be available for larger-scale and impact projects).

You can read more about the NCSU Alt-Textbook project and review our call for proposals on the Alt-Textbook Project website or you can contact us with questions at: wmcross@ncsu.edu.

We look forward to hearing from you!

Figure 6.2 | **Alt-Textbook Call for Proposals**

Alt-Textbook Rubric

I. Please rank the proposals on a scale from 1 – 5:

(**1** = poor quality, **2** = low quality, **3** = solid quality,
4 = high quality, **5** = outstanding proposal)

Cost Savings: Does the proposal describe materials that will not require students to spend money or, if an existing textbook is being used, materials that significantly reduce the cost to students?

_____ Proposal one   _____ Proposal two

Pedagogical Innovation: Does the proposal describe materials that do something innovative, that a traditional print textbook could not?

_____ Proposal one   _____ Proposal two

Impact: Does the proposal describe materials that will benefit many students at NCSU and/or benefit students and instructors across the field at many institutions? Will the materials be sustainable over multiple courses and multiple semesters?

_____ Proposal one   _____ Proposal two

Ability to Succeed: Does the proposal describe materials that could reasonably be created or adopted for the 2016-17 academic year? Does it adequately describe logistics and identify resources within or beyond the Libraries that can help the instructor meet any challenges posed by the proposal such as technical needs, licensing, support, etc.

_____ Proposal one   _____ Proposal two

II. Please rank all proposals based on their priority for funding and what level of funding is appropriate:

$500 = a small pilot project

$1,000 = a large, innovative, or high-impact project

$2,000 = an outstanding project that will serve many students or significantly advance pedagogy

Group A: These proposals should definitely be funded:

_____

_____

_____

Group B: These proposals should be funded if resources are available, in rank order:

_____

_____

_____

Group C: These proposals need more work before we are comfortable funding them:

_____

_____

_____

Figure 6.3 | **Alt-Textbook Proposal Evaluation Rubric**

The cost savings created by an alt-textbook program were one major focus for our program. We were deeply concerned that more than half of college students cannot afford their assigned textbooks and that more than one in ten fail a course for this reason.[7] As a STEM-focused, public land-grant institution, we were also alarmed that many students report being unable to pursue majors in "expensive" subjects like science and engineering, particularly first-generation students and those from underrepresented populations, students whom these fields can least afford to lose.[8] To address these concerns, we designed our Alt-Textbook program to attract instructors using expensive textbooks in hopes of supporting them in transitioning to free alternatives.

The NCSU Libraries also understood our Alt-Textbook project as an opportunity to leverage technology and library expertise to facilitate teaching and learning. OERs can be both "free and better" than closed textbooks because they are available to all students and they leverage digital resources.[9] Scholars have compared the move from print to digital OERs to the transition from rotary telephones to smartphones: not only are the new tools more effective for their original purpose, but they enable new practices to develop. In the same way, we designed the program to solicit projects based on course readings, but also projects that used multimedia resources, collaborative digital discussion spaces, and other methods and that enable new types of teaching and learning.

We also believe that the library is "uniquely positioned to work with faculty on curricular change" as a fertile space for collaboration with campus partners, and due to the unique types of expertise available in libraries that can complement an instructor's deep subject-based knowledge.[10] Library expertise in instructional design, digital resources and literacy, and copyright can help instructors create OERs that transcend the sorts of textbooks that leave many feeling like "hired hands" rather than partners with their students in learning.[11]

In order to meet our objectives of addressing equity issues and advancing teaching and learning, the NCSU Libraries gathered a committee of librarians that represented diverse types of expertise. We highlighted expertise in a variety of areas including instructional design, digital literacy, collections, digital tools and development, copyright and fair use analysis, electronic resources and course reserves, scholarly communication and publishing, and OERs, as well as diverse subject specialties. This committee worked collaboratively to develop outreach materials, present workshops on open education, and, most significantly, serve as liaisons to the faculty awardees. As applications arrive, the Alt-Textbook team considers potential issues or roadblocks that each may face if they were to be developed. Some may require extra assistance with web hosting or making materials available via course reserves, while others may not have enough information to specify which digital tool or platform would be best to use.

This liaison relationship is at the heart of the Alt-Textbook project. Based on the subject area of the grant and any potential issues identified, each grant awardee is assigned a library liaison from the Alt-Textbook project team. The liaison answers questions, tracks progress, and acts as a point of contact that connects awardees with the libraries' services and resources. This team-based approach gives all library staff a stake in the project and spotlights library services and expertise. Librarians across the institution reported new interest in services like electronic reserves, an example of instructional support very familiar to librarians but novel for several instructors, as well as consultations and library instruction.

Similarly, our funding model was designed to both reduce costs for students and galvanize better practice. Unlike OER projects where the library disburses funds primarily intended as a "carrot" to incentivize better behavior by using existing material, our intention was to use funds to empower instructors to redesign or create new materials. In the first two rounds, instructors have requested and used funds to do everything from hiring graduate student assistants for content development and web design to paying to make resources available with fewer restrictions.

"Your Materials to Support Your Teaching": Launching the Project

These two principles—collaborative action and support for innovation—were the hallmarks of the Alt-Textbook project as we launched the first round in 2014. We publicized the program widely in partnership with individual departments and colleges, our subject specialists, and the Office of Faculty Development. Our outreach included informational e-mails, a press release, an art box on our web page, coverage in our campus newspaper, and a series of information sessions in the libraries and as part of existing event series with our campus partners.

Our outreach was successful, generating a diverse set of proposals from fourteen faculty members from the sciences, social sciences, humanities, and professional programs. The majority of departments were represented, with the College of Education offering the largest number of proposals. We also received proposals from our Chancellor's Faculty Excellence Program "Cluster Hires"—faculty members recruited to NCSU to work on interdisciplinary issues such as data-driven science and the digital transformation of education.[12]

We brought together a campus-wide committee to review the grant proposals. This campus committee included librarians, faculty members, administrators, and an undergraduate student. The campus committee evaluated all applications thoroughly and announced nine winners for the first round. The awardees' disciplines ranged from biotechnology to statistics, from counseling to foreign languages. Each awardee was assigned a liaison from the Alt-Textbook committee based on anticipated needs. For example, instructors planning to use openly licensed materials or rely on fair use for video clips were matched with the libraries' Copyright and Digital Scholarship Center. Those developing digital tools or using code-sharing repositories like GitHub were matched with a representative from the Digital Library Initiatives Department. Those leveraging the university's student-facing content management system (Moodle) worked with Access and Delivery Services staff.

After the committee evaluates the grants, faculty awardees are invited to an Alt-Textbook orientation. This offers the libraries another opportunity to raise awareness about our collections, liaisons, and established services like electronic reserves and licensed videos. Orientation provides faculty and Alt-Textbook liaisons the opportunity to meet face-to-face to discuss plans for their OER, develop time lines, address questions or concerns moving forward, and to set up further consultation. Awardees expressed appreciation for the orientation, and several specifically mentioned the value of discovering library services they had not been aware of previously.

Awardees also began to form a community of practice around the Alt-Textbook project. In addition to regular discussion with their library liaisons and consultations with other librarians, they also requested that the libraries host regular gatherings for them to discuss their projects as well as larger questions about instructional design and pedagogy. These optional meetings were fruitful both as a venue for awardees to consider logistical issues, such as managing funds and working with graduate students, and to learn about new ways to approach teaching based on perspectives from beyond their disciplines. With a deeper understanding of the libraries' resources and services and the funds to put their plans into action, the instructors developed their resources using the same principles of collaborative action in service of innovative instruction that are at the heart of the Alt-Textbook project.

Alt-Textbooks in Action

The creation, application, and evaluation of alt-textbook projects involved many parties. We in the libraries offered ourselves as resources and coordinated with other university partners invested in teaching and learning such as the Office of Faculty Development and Distance Education & Learning Technology Applications (DELTA) to provide support, but fundamentally the success of Alt-Textbooks requires instructors and learners.

We also considered a variety of approaches to the ownership and licensing of the alt-texts. Under NCSU's copyright policy, faculty own traditional non-directed works unless they make "exceptional use of university resources."[13] In the early rounds, we made the decision not to assert any claims to institutional ownership of the projects, beyond a standard nonexclusive license to use them. As a result, we are free to post the projects on the libraries' site and use them in other campus and promotional contexts, but faculty retain the right to the works they created.

We also took a balanced approach to openly licensing the final alt-texts. In our general introduction to open education we explained the value of fully open materials in the "5 R" (retain, reuse, revise, remix, and redistribute) sense of the term.[14] We also described the way that a Creative Commons license is traditionally used to create the legal framework for this open sharing. In order to provide flexibility for faculty experimenting with a variety of approaches to course design, however, we permitted openness to take a variety of forms. This understanding of openness as a spectrum gave our faculty members space to experiment and incorporate fair use in a more robust manner.

As a result, all projects have a public face that is open in the most complete sense so that others around the world can benefit from the project. But in some cases that meant a flexible approach where readings and syllabi were listed, rather than the full text of all materials. This compromise approach made the early rounds more attractive for faculty and permitted a richer and more experimental approach for instructors just dipping their toes into OER creation. In later rounds, however, we have strengthened our commitment to openness in the fullest sense. As the project's reputation has grown on campus, and our own expertise in the libraries has grown, we are better positioned to support projects that are innovative but also truly open to the world.

The stories of the creation, application, and evaluation of alt-texts that follow provide some examples of the diverse ways that instructors have worked with others, including their students, to try to ensure that alt-texts add value to the academic experience. In all of these cases, the librarian liaisons offered assistance to the instructors and their students in identifying relevant open resources, but that was generally only the beginning of creating the alt-texts.

Involving Students in the Creating of Alt-Texts

Instructors have engaged students with two approaches to creating alt-texts: advanced preparation and active learning. In the advanced preparation approach, instructors hire a graduate student or advanced undergraduate student to work with them in the development of an alt-text, typically during the semester prior to when the course is scheduled to be taught. This type of working with student(s) takes some of the burden off the instructor while creating an environment to discuss issues around the selection of relevant resources. For the student developer, it builds their resume and potentially inspires the next generation of instructors to consider developing or using new types of texts in their teaching. Regardless of the subsequent impact of the alt-text on the learners in the course, learning took place in crafting course materials with the advanced student and instructor as potential co-learners, depending on the nature of the work.

Another type of creative engagement occurs when part of the alt-text is created by the students taking the course under the direction of the instructor as part of the active learning in the course. In some cases, such as the development of chemistry laboratory videos by Maria Gallardo-Williams, the students in the course participated but were not graded on their participation.[15] The most integrated approach involves students in creation and evaluation, and much of the learning in the course is self-directed and active through these processes. An example of this is the student-driven biotechnology OER created through a project by Sabrina Robertson and Carlos Goller's (Biotechnology) BIT 410/510: Core Technologies in Molecular Biology students. In biotechnology, methodologies evolve rapidly, and traditional textbooks often become outdated even before making it to print. The BIT OER is a dynamic online educational platform for all things biotechnology-related.[16] The unique content on this site was created and evaluated by teams of students working together to provide an innovative, freely accessible educational resource for the local, national, and international biotechnology community.

Evaluating the Use of Alt-Texts

Methods to evaluate traditional course materials have been used to measure the impact of alt-texts and perhaps provide information at a more granular level. For example, replacing a textbook with digital course reserve readings can reveal what information students have accessed or downloaded. An instructor using a traditional textbook might never know whether a student purchased or opened the required text, but a project using readings in a course reserves system offers the instructor information on whether students logged into the system and how many times certain readings were accessed or downloaded. In the NCSU Libraries reserves system, instructors can use the Statistics heading to see a link labeled Student Usage, which represents total views and total unique students who have accessed each item. Educational materials linked to Moodle or other learning management systems can provide similar statistics. Instructors have ensured the use of alt-texts through their design of activities during the course that requires learners to interact with the resource through homework, quizzes, exams, or papers. Some open textbooks and alt-text resources from large OER providers like OpenStax have built-in assessment components, and the NCSU Libraries project may explore this in the future.

A few instructors pursued research to compare the effectiveness of their alt-text resources with other strategies as part of their commitment to growing the Scholarship of Teaching and Learning.[17] Although significant research has been done on the efficacy of OERs in other contexts, it can be challenging to tease out the differences related to simply changing content and format apart from the complexity of changing the overall learner experience through the project design, greater involvement with and cocreation of the materials, and novelty for the instructor.[18] Class evaluations used at NCSU for lecture and laboratory courses ask the following question about course readings: "The course readings were valuable aids to learning" on a five-point Likert-type scale from Strongly Agree to Strongly Disagree, with an additional choice of Not Applicable. At NCSU, the Office of Institutional Research and Planning, which coordinates the course evaluation process, also invites instructors, departments, and colleges to develop and add up to seven closed-ended questions and six additional open-ended questions which can be used to address special interests or instructional innovations. This is an avenue to potentially ask specific questions about the value of the material. Although cost savings are an important driver, students may not realize that they have saved money due to the use of the alt-text unless it is for a large course where other sections or students from previous years have discussed the cost of the typical textbook.

Reflecting on the Utility of Alt-Texts

There are many viewpoints on the utility of alt-texts. While those of student and instructor in the context of the specific course come most readily to mind, taking the vantage point of the academic department, the university, the community of instructors who teach similar courses, or potential learners outside the university can tell powerful stories.

For instructors, whether tenure-track, teaching faculty pursuing promotion, or tenured, it is worth reflecting on the investment in developing an alt-text and measuring its local and potentially global impact. Reflection is one way to understand how the time spent developing the resource compared to the effort initially proposed in the grant, and to budget time effectively in future efforts. Having been awarded a grant for a teaching-related activity is an important item for annual activity reports or progress reports. The benefits of developing closer relationships with library staff carry over to other courses and projects. Instructors have parlayed the ideas and materials created with Alt-Textbook funds into inspiring other faculty in their departments to join in to pursue additional resources. For example, Gallardo-Williams, a grant recipient in 2014 for her nationally recognized Student-Made Audiovisuals Reinforcing Techniques (S.M.A.R.T.) lab videos, subsequently earned a grant from the Office of Faculty Development to purchase software for additional works that resulted in a paper that she coauthored with students in the *Journal of Chemical Education*.[19]

For the broader learning community, impact varies tremendously depending on how available and discoverable the alt-materials are and how many students take the course or study the subject. For example, projects housed entirely in the NCSU Libraries course reserves are limited to students enrolled in the specific course at NCSU. Alt-text materials housed on the open Web or on a faculty or NCSU website are discoverable by Google and other search engines, but someone has to be looking for them. Statistics about the numbers of visitors, downloads, or links has been tracked by adding Google Analytics or other tools to the site management. Placing alt-materials on the open Web in a known repository with a wide audience base garners the most traffic. The S.M.A.R.T. lab videos were uploaded to YouTube in addition to an NCSU server. Posting to a public site may provide both a hosting solution and very compelling evidence about the number of views. For example, the YouTube–hosted video "Drying with Anhydrous Sodium Sulfate" posted in 2015 had 3,512 views as of July 26, 2016. The evaluative practices described above offer insight into the benefits of alt-texts for teaching and learning. Additionally, the libraries have seen significant benefits from the project.

OPENING MANY DOORS TO THE LIBRARIES

The Alt-Textbook project encourages NCSU instructors to create digital, multimedia learning materials that reflect their individual voices and teaching styles. In addition to our well-known role of pooling resources to create efficient, university-wide access to scholarly content, the project spotlights the libraries' collections, services, and expertise in new specialty areas. It demonstrates how we contribute to our campus community's success in a variety of ways, making the work of libraries, and of librarians, more visible. The NCSU Libraries' strategic plan includes the Alt-Textbook project as an integral way that the libraries are enhancing student success, which is also a university strategic goal.[20]

Information sessions, the orientation, and the projects themselves provide a context for the libraries to introduce open culture more broadly to the university community. Instructors who attend the information sessions strengthen their awareness of librarians' expertise. They learn that librarians can consult with them on specific competency areas as they navigate building their own OERs regardless of whether they apply for or succeed with an Alt-Textbook award application. The Alt-Textbook initiative often attracts instructors looking to do innovative work, and librarian liaisons are able to develop relationships that can lead to further library collaboration. By shining a light on how the library can support teaching, learning, and research, we set a foundation for collaboration beyond the Alt-Textbook initiative. Individual projects have served as powerful case studies for cross-cutting libraries services like the Makerspace and the Copyright and Digital Scholarship Center. Past Alt-Textbook projects have led to faculty presenting at conferences or publishing articles, further disseminating this work.

The intended audience of the Alt-Textbook promotion is much broader than the instructors eligible to apply for the program. Hosting several information sessions each semester about the Alt-Textbook program has not only promoted the program, but introduced the idea of OERs to the broader university community and all who visit the NCSU Libraries website. Seeing the announcements and facts about the textbook problem exposes audiences to both the Alt-Textbook grants and the possibilities that come with utilizing OERs regardless of whether they attend a session. They may spark ideas for administrators and course coordinators to discuss partnering with other instructors in their department or program to promote wider adoption of alt-texts across course sections which can lead to more savings. Inviting key stakeholders to participate on the selection committee is another avenue to creating broader awareness of OERs and what instructors need in order to develop them.

The Alt-Textbook project was further promoted by the libraries' External Relations staff and the Web Team. A Web presence[21] on the NCSU Libraries website was established, which provided a space to list the projects from the first year and to discuss the textbook problem. Branding was designed for the project to be used in press releases, social media, and the libraries' home page "art box" for promotional purposes.

The External Relations team further assisted in creating several GIFs and social media posts to promote the project on social media and on library and campus electronic signage.

The Alt-Textbook program also became an NCSU Libraries "Library Story."[22] Library Stories offers librarians and their partners, typically faculty and students, an opportunity to share examples of their innovative, collaborative projects.[23] Since much of the work taking place in librarianship is done "behind the curtain," librarian portraits and links to staff pages are highlighted in every Library Story to associate the library with those who work within. This helps to make what can sometimes feel like invisible work more visible. The Alt-Textbook Library Story was featured prominently on the libraries home page and shared through social media. Additionally, the program was featured in the NCSU student newspaper, and in *Library Journal.*[24]

Promoting the project through marketing and communications has helped not only to raise awareness of the program, but also to demonstrate to students our proactive attitude toward addressing textbook costs, and to make instructors aware of the expertise and opportunities that the libraries provide. By opening another door to the libraries and the expertise of the staff within, we have responded to the demand for affordable textbooks while reaffirming the central role of the library as a hub for collaboration and as an agent of change.

CONCLUSION: AN ONGOING PROJECT

Open education gives libraries an opportunity to meet our mission by making resources available in the service of our patrons and the public good. Librarians around the world are answering this call. As we work to transform education, we should not miss a parallel opportunity to transform the way the academy understands libraries and librarianship. The success of our pilot Alt-Textbook project led to ongoing funding from the NCSU Libraries administration, which was impressed with the innovative work and the national attention.

Our second round, launched in 2015, included more projects supported by a new cohort of library liaisons. It also connected with new library programs and services, including work in our Makerspace on 3D printing of bone samples for a veterinary anatomy class and our visualization services for digital history projects, as well as deeper work with librarians who are now familiar with the power of open education. We attracted a libraries fellow to work on the project, expanding its reach and filling in gaps in support and sustainability from prior years. As of this writing, the program's third round is in development, and it promises to be even more impactful and exciting.

The reach of the project, however, extends far beyond the individual alt-texts. Through these efforts, the libraries have built new relationships with many innovative and dynamic faculty members and launched new projects built on those relationships. We have also developed a trusted relationship with our campus bookstore and university system press, and with a national set of libraries working in this area. The bookstore has been a critical partner in many of the libraries' efforts to address the textbook problem, including our textbook purchasing program and offering print-on-demand service for our Open Physics Textbook. With the Alt-Textbook project, the bookstore has continued to offer print-on-demand options for all digital works as well as sharing information about assigned alt-texts for students looking to acquire books for the semester. We are also working on larger data-sharing efforts to identify potential candidates for Alt-Textbook outreach, as well as general information for students about comparison shopping and textbook options. Similarly, the UNC Press has been an outstanding partner, supporting our work with their expertise and collaborating on grants and innovative projects around platforms and support for OER creation.

Overall, the project has sparked fruitful conversations about the value of open culture with many stakeholders—from undergraduates to state legisla-tors—that years of advocacy around open access could not reach. By opening our doors to open education, the NCSU Libraries has introduced ourselves and our work in a whole new way.

Notes

1. College Board, "Trends in College Pricing" (2014), https://secure-media.collegeboard .org/digitalServices/misc/trends/2014-trends-college-pricing-report-final.pdf.
2. Government Accountability Office, "College Textbooks: Students Have Access to Textbook Information" (2013), www.gao.gov/assets/660/655066.pdf.
3. There are varying opinions on whether this is a constructive service, as summarized by Rick Anderson (https://scholarlykitchen.sspnet.org/2016/07/07/academic-libraries -and-the-textbook-taboo-time-to-get-over-it/) and Steven Bell. We discuss some of these issues, as well as our other early efforts, in G. Raschke, and S. Shanks, "Water on a Hot Skillet: Textbooks, Open Educational Resources, and the Role of the Library," in *The No Shelf Required Guide to E-Book Purchasing*, ed. S. Polanka (Chicago: ALA TechSource, 2011), 52–57, http://lj.libraryjournal.com/2013/10/opinion/steven-bell/ openness-to-textbooks-alternatives-is-growing-from-the-bell-tower/.
4. For more discussion of the project, see Jill Laster, "North Carolina State U. Gives Students Free Access to Physics Textbook Online" (February 12, 2010), www.chronicle .com/blogs/wiredcampus/north-carolina-state-u-gives-students-free-access-to-physics -textbook-online/21238.
5. See http://sites.temple.edu/alttextbook/, discussed in Nick DeSantis, "Temple U. Project Ditches Textbooks for Homemade Digital Alternatives" (February 7, 2012), www .chronicle.com/blogs/wiredcampus/temple-project-ditches-textbooks-for-homemade -digital-alternatives/35247; "Alt-Textbook Project," NCSU Libraries, www.lib .ncsu.edu/alttextbook.
6. "List of North American OER Policies & Projects," SPARC, http://sparcopen.org/ our-work/list-of-oer-policies-projects/; "UMASS Library Open Education Initiative," UMass Amherst Libraries, www.library.umass.edu/services/teaching-and-learning/oer/ open-education-initiative/.
7. U.S. PIRG Education Fund and the Student PIRGS, "Fixing the Broken Textbook Market" (2014), www.uspirg.org/reports/usp/fixing-broken-textbook-market.
8. Doug Ward, "Why You Ought to Think Twice before Assigning a Pricey Textbook," *Chronicle of Higher Education* (September 9, 2015), htttp://chronicle.com/article/ Why-You-Ought-to-Think-Twice-/232877/.
9. ELI Webinar: "Searching for 'Free and Better': Evaluating the Efficacy of Open Educational Resources," Educause, 2015, www.educause.edu/eli/events/eli-annual -meeting/2015/searching-free-and-better-evaluating-efficacy-open-educational -resources.

10. Joan Lippincott, Anu Vedantham, and Kim Duckett, "Libraries as Enablers of Pedagogical and Curricular Change," *Educause Review* (2014), http://er.educause .edu/articles/2014/10/libraries-as-enablers-of-pedagogical-and-curricular-change.

11. Will Cross, "Library Expertise Driving Pedagogical Innovation: The Role of Libraries in Bringing 'Open' to the Classroom and to the World," in *Open Access and the Future of Scholarly Communication*, ed. Kevin L. Smith and Katherine A. Dickson (Washington, DC: Rowman and Littlefield, 2016).

12. For more information about NCSU cluster hires, see https://workthatmatters.ncsu.edu/.

13. See NCSU's Copyright Regulation 1.25.03, https://policies.ncsu.edu/regulation/reg-01 –25–03.

14. David Wiley, "The Access Compromise and the 5th R," http://opencontent.org/blog/ archives/3221.

15. "S.M.A.R.T. Lab Videos," Undergraduate Organic Chemistry Teaching Laboratories, North Carolina State University, www.ncsu.edu/chemistry/octl/lab-videos.html.

16. "Open Educational Resource," Biotechnology, North Carolina State University, http:// biotech.ncsu.edu/projects.

17. NC State, Office of Faculty Development, "Scholarship of Teaching & Learning," https://ofd.ncsu.edu/scholarship-and-research/scholarship-of-teaching-learning/.

18. Lane Fischer, John Hilton III, T. Jared Robinson, and David A. Wiley, "A Multi-Institutional Study of the Impact of Open Textbook Adoption on the Learning Outcomes of Post-Secondary Students," *Journal of Computing in Higher Education* 27, no. 3 (2015): 159–72.

19. Maria Gallardo-Williams, NC State Undergraduate Organic Chemistry Teaching Laboratories—S.M.A.R.T. Lab Videos, www.youtube.com/channel/UCr1PT0Jduc MG1-SP8hpt18A; Jeremy T. Jordan, Melinda C. Box, Kristen E. Eguren, Thomas A. Parker, Victoria M. Saraldi-Gallardo, Michael I. Wolfe, and Maria T. Gallardo-Williams, "Effectiveness of Student-Generated Video as a Teaching Tool for an Instrumental Technique in the Organic Chemistry Laboratory," *Journal of Chemical Education* 93, no. 1 (2016): 141–45.

20. "NCSU Libraries Strategic Plan, FY 2016/17 to FY2019/20," NCSU Libraries, www .lib.ncsu.edu/about/strategic-plan.

21. "Alt-Textbook Project," NCSU Libraries, www.lib.ncsu.edu/alttextbook.

22. "NCSU Libraries Library Stories," NCSU Libraries, www.lib.ncsu.edu/stories/alt -textbooks-saving-students-money-and-supporting-innovative-teaching.

23. Chris Vitiello, "NC State's 'Library Stories' Publicize Librarians' Innovative Collabora- tions," *Marketing Library Services* 30, no. 2, (2016).

24. Samuel Griffin, "Program Cuts Textbook Prices, Involves Students," The Technician (February 1, 2016), www.technicianonline.com/features/article_317206f2-c8a4–11e5

-a906–5b93b1a3e3b4.html; Lisa Peet, "NCSU Libraries Spur Innovation through Alt-Textbook Grants," *Library Journal* (September 11, 2014), lj.libraryjournal .com/2014/09/oa/ncsu-libraries-spur-innovation-through-alt-textbook-grants.

BIBLIOGRAPHY

"Alt-Textbook Project." NCSU Libraries. www.lib.ncsu.edu/alttextbook.

College Board. "Trends in College Pricing." 2014. https://secure-media.collegeboard.org/ digitalServices/misc/trends/2014-trends-college-pricing-report-final.pdf.

Cross, Will, "Library Expertise Driving Pedagogical Innovation: The Role of Libraries in Bringing 'Open' to the Classroom and to the World." In *Open Access and the Future of Scholarly Communication: Implementation*, edited by Kevin. L. Smith and Katherine A. Dickson, 71–97. Washington, DC: Rowman and Littlefield, 2016.

Fischer, Lane, John Hilton III, T. Jared Robinson, and David A. Wiley. "A Multi-Institutional Study of the Impact of Open Textbook Adoption on the Learning Outcomes of Post-Secondary Students." *Journal of Computing in Higher Education* 27, no. 3 (2015): 159–72.

Gallardo-Williams, Maria. NC State Undergraduate Organic Chemistry Teaching Laboratories—S.M.A.R.T. Lab Videos. www.youtube.com/channel/UCr1PT0Jduc MG1-SP8hpt18A.

Government Accountability Office. "College Textbooks: Students Have Access to Textbook Information." 2013. www.gao.gov/assets/660/655066.pdf.

Griffin, Samuel. "Program Cuts Textbook Prices, Involves Students." The Technician. February 1, 2016. www.technicianonline.com/features/article_317206f2-c8a4–11e5 -a906–5b93b1a3e3b4.html.

Jordan, Jeremy T., Melinda C. Box, Kristen E. Eguren, Thomas A. Parker, Victoria M. Saraldi-Gallardo, Michael I. Wolfe, and Maria T. Gallardo-Williams. "Effectiveness of Student-Generated Video as a Teaching Tool for an Instrumental Technique in the Organic Chemistry Laboratory." *Journal of Chemical Education* 93, no. 1 (2016): 141–45.

"List of North American OER Policies & Projects." SPARC. http://sparcopen.org/our -work/list-of-oer-policies-projects/.

NC State Office of Faculty Development. "Scholarship of Teaching & Learning." https:// ofd.ncsu.edu/scholarship-and-research/scholarship-of-teaching-learning/.

"NCSU Libraries Library Stories." NCSU Libraries. www.lib.ncsu.edu/stories/alt-textbooks -saving-students-money-and-supporting-innovative-teaching.

"NCSU Libraries Strategic Plan, FY 2016/17 to FY2019/20." NCSU Libraries. www.lib
.ncsu.edu/about/strategic-plan.

"Open Educational Resource." Biotechnology. North Carolina State University. http://
biotech.ncsu.edu/projects.

Peet, Lisa. "NCSU Libraries Spur Innovation through Alt-Textbook Grants." *Library
Journal,* September 11, 2014. lj.libraryjournal.com/2014/09/oa/ncsu-libraries-spur
-innovation-through-alt-textbook-grants.

"S.M.A.R.T. Lab Videos." Undergraduate Organic Chemistry Teaching Laboratories. North
Carolina State University. www.ncsu.edu/chemistry/octl/lab-videos.html.

"UMASS Library Open Education Initiative." UMass Amherst Libraries. www.library
.umass.edu/services/teaching-and-learning/oer/open-education-initiative/.

Vitiello, Chris. "NC State's 'Library Stories' Publicize Librarians' Innovative Collaborations."
Marketing Library Services 30, no. 2 (2016): 1–4.

CONNECTING LIBRARY TEXTBOOK PROGRAMS TO CAMPUS INITIATIVES

Josh Cromwell

In recent years, many academic libraries have been exploring the potential of open textbooks. However, due to budget shortfalls and a general unfamiliarity with open textbooks on many campuses, some libraries have found it difficult to establish and launch such a program on their campus. These libraries have had to think creatively about other avenues for securing the necessary funding and support to make their plan a reality. In particular, libraries that have been able to clearly demonstrate how open textbooks align with other campus initiatives and broader university goals have had more success in getting buy-in from administrators and the campus community. This chapter will examine the Open Textbook Initiative at the University of Southern Mississippi as a case study demonstrating the importance of building partnerships and aligning the initiative with the university's mission. The chapter will conclude by offering some lessons learned from the initiative that can be implemented on other campuses.

BACKGROUND

In 2013, the Mississippi Legislature voted to allow the State Institutions of Higher Learning (IHL) Board of Trustees to implement a new funding model for the institutions of higher learning in the state. Whereas the old model allocated funding based on a fixed percentage, the new formula utilized current enrollment numbers as well as the number of credit hours completed, thereby placing a high premium on both recruiting new students and on ensuring that those students remained enrolled.[1] This created a significant challenge for Southern Miss, because the university had to develop a strategy to bolster enrollment and retention in order to secure needed funding while also addressing the challenges that many prospective students face, particularly rising tuition costs and other expenses. To this end, the university established a number of initiatives specifically targeted toward student success, including the creation of a Student Success Center, which served as a centralized location where students could go when they needed assistance. The university also established a new position, the associate provost for academic excellence, who was tasked with the responsibility of overseeing student success initiatives.

In light of this new emphasis, the University Libraries began considering a series of strategies intended to align the library's mission with new broader campus initiatives. Librarians developed a student success collection designed to help students improve their study habits or cope with stress. Others also developed librarian-led workshops on similar topics. However, others within the libraries began exploring the concept of open textbooks or open educational resources and found that an OER program had the potential to be beneficial to students while also aligning the library with campus student success initiatives.

WHY OPEN TEXTBOOKS?

Ultimately, the library determined to pursue an open textbook program for three major reasons: cost savings for students, the library's existing capability to support the program, and the ability to support campus-wide student success initiatives. The cost of traditional textbooks has long been a significant burden for many students and thus is an obvious barrier to success.[2] At Southern Miss, 51.7 percent of full-time undergraduates during the 2015–16 academic year were awarded some form of need-based financial aid, and on average, this aid only met 67 percent of the financial need of these students.[3] Introducing an open textbook program on campus provided an excellent way to alleviate part of this financial burden on the student population by replacing expensive traditional textbooks with free open textbooks.

Aside from the benefits of open textbooks for students, library leadership identified two other benefits to an open textbook program. The library has an existing infrastructure in place to support the textbook collection, both in terms of technology and personnel. The university's institutional repository, Aquila, is managed by the library and offers an ideal platform for storing the completed textbooks. Aquila is optimized for discoverability, meaning that the textbook collection can easily be discovered and utilized by faculty at other institutions as well, further broadening the benefits of the books. Furthermore, the library was already a campus leader in promoting open access through workshops and events such as Open Access Week each year, so librarians possessed the necessary knowledge to assist faculty in identifying resources for inclusion in open textbooks.

Most importantly for this discussion, an open textbook program provided the library with a perfect opportunity to align itself with the university's campus objectives. As academic library budgets continue to shrink on many campuses, it is becoming more important than ever for libraries to demonstrate their value to the university. As Rick Anderson has discussed recently, libraries that have been able to provide demonstrable examples of how their activities and services support the university's goals tend to have much more success in obtaining the needed resources from university administration to implement those services.[4] By launching an open textbook program, the library was positioned to directly support university initiatives for student success by lowering costs for students, thus making it easier for students to enroll or stay enrolled in the university. And by increasing access to open textbooks, the library could give students a greater chance to perform better in their classes than their counterparts who could not afford to buy required texts.

FORMING PARTNERSHIPS

After outlining the benefits of pursuing an open textbook program, library leaders began focusing on identifying strategic partners who could assist in promoting and launching the program. The first step was getting buy-in from the university administration. This meant that it was imperative to demonstrate the value of a library-led OER initiative in supporting the university's mission and goals, a case that libraries are already accustomed to making with other initiatives, such as their institutional repositories.[5] Furthermore, a partnership at the administrative level provided the chance to secure additional funding for the faculty grants that would be a key component in launching the program. To this end a group of library representatives met with the newly hired associate provost for academic excellence to discuss the idea. The associate provost had already taken part in discussions about other possible avenues for collaboration between the provost's office and the library, such as possibly relocating the Student Success Center to the library, so this existing relationship provided the perfect opportunity to propose the open textbook idea. Furthermore, because the new associate provost was responsible for overseeing student success, she was the most logical potential partner because of all of the goals that the two programs had in common. After discussing the idea, the associate provost agreed that the proposal's goals did align well with several of the objectives of her office and she agreed to cosponsor the program. This meant that the Provost's Office agreed to provide 50 percent of the funding necessary for the open textbook program while the University Libraries provided the other half.

Upon getting the associate provost's support, the library next explored the opportunity to partner with the campus's Learning Enhancement Center (LEC), which focused on instructional technology, distance learning, and other resources for faculty. While librarians were well prepared to assist faculty with identifying resources and with understanding the basics of copyright, open access, and fair use, they were less familiar with some of the available campus technologies that could be incorporated into the books and with assuring that the textbooks complied with accessibility standards. Thus, with the associate provost's backing, the library reached out to LEC staff to gauge their willingness to provide some of the training that faculty participants in the program would need.

After the LEC agreed to support the program, the library explored opportunities to partner with faculty members to spread the word about the initiative. The proposed plan was presented to the university's Textbook and Course Materials Advisory Committee[6] and to the campus bookstore to ensure that all parties understood what the proposal entailed and to address any questions that the two groups had. Once this was accomplished, the library and the associate provost began reaching out to faculty who were either already using some type of OER in their courses or who were seeking out more information on open textbooks. The two groups discovered that many faculty members were only nominally familiar with open textbooks, but many were open to the idea of learning more about OER and were sympathetic to the plight of their students regarding the high costs of many traditional textbooks. With faculty now familiar with the plan and with the necessary partnerships in place, the library formed a committee to implement the program and to ready it for introduction across campus.

THE OPEN TEXTBOOK INITIATIVE AT SOUTHERN MISS

The Open Textbook Initiative (OTI) was officially introduced to faculty in fall 2015. The proposal for the OTI was adapted from the model used at the University of Massachusetts at Amherst. Marilyn Billings, scholarly communication and special initiatives librarian and founder of the open textbook program at UMass Amherst, visited the campus in April 2015 and led a presentation on their Open Education Initiative,[7] which was then in its fifth year and had cumulatively saved UMass Amherst students approximately $1,100,000 in textbook costs to that point.[8] In the days following that presentation, the library leadership determined that a slightly adapted version of the UMass Amherst model was the best approach for Southern Miss, and Billings graciously agreed to offer advice during the planning stages as well.

Once a model was agreed upon, the next step was to outline the terms and criteria for the initiative. Ultimately, the planning committee decided upon a three-tiered system of grants in which faculty would apply for one of the three tiers that they deemed most appropriate to their needs. In the initial tier ("Adopt"), recipients were awarded $400 and were required to adopt an existing open textbook to replace the commercial textbook previously used in the course. This was the most basic of the three models and thus carried the smallest cash award. Nonetheless, it offered faculty an incentive to move away from expensive textbooks toward an open alternative, with the intent that this tier would appeal to faculty who were interested in open textbooks conceptually but who did not have time to create their own.

For the second tier ("Modify"), faculty members received an $800 award and were instructed to create an open textbook or course pack using a combination of existing open textbooks, library resources, and other materials that they could incorporate into the books without violating copyright or licensing agreements. This tier offered a more substantial grant than the first model since the faculty member had to invest a significant amount of time to compile and organize the various resources that they would include in their textbook. While this tier provided the added benefit of developing a textbook that was more directly tailored to the associated course, it still did not require the same level of commitment as creating a fully original textbook.

The final tier ("Create") offered faculty the chance to completely build their own open textbook, which would be housed in the institutional repository upon completion. Because of the much greater workload, this tier offered the most substantial monetary grant of the three, with each recipient receiving $1,600. The "Create" tier also offered faculty the greatest degree of flexibility. By creating their own book, faculty had the freedom to completely customize the book to correspond with all of the themes and objectives they intended to cover in the course. So while this tier clearly presented faculty with the largest workload, it was designed to offer the greatest level of incentive for those willing to make the commitment that this tier required.

Once the tiers were finalized, the committee next turned to establishing an application for faculty who wanted to participate in the initiative. The first step was to identify a list of criteria that clearly outlined the eligibility requirements for the initiative. These included:

- A clear proposal for replacing a required commercial textbook with a freely available open textbook (replacing a textbook used for multiple courses strengthens the application)
- An explanation of how the proposed project meets the outcomes of the initiative and of the course(s)
- The estimated savings to Southern Miss students
- The potential for the project to be implemented in the 2016–17 academic year
- The inclusion of a clear plan to assess student learning in the course
- An indication of which tier (Adopt, Modify, Create) the faculty member wishes to use

In addition to these basic criteria, there were also a few other qualifiers. For instance, faculty who had already adopted open textbooks or faculty who were seeking to use a textbook rental program as opposed to a fully open textbook would not be eligible for the program. The committee also required that faculty who were selected to receive the grants must attend a series of training opportunities that would provide recipients with a better understanding of open textbooks, along with a series of best practices and other suggestions for developing and implementing the books. The application also stated that the grant could be applied to any course offered at the university, but that courses that are part of the General Education Curriculum would receive additional consideration, because those courses are required for all students and thus hold the potential to benefit a much larger group of students than upper-level discipline-specific courses.

Given these criteria, faculty members were then instructed to apply by submitting the following information:

- The full name, title, department, and e-mail of the applicant
- Course information (including number, title, size of enrollment, frequency of offering, current textbook and its cost)
- A narrative (500 words) addressing interest in doing the project, background (if any) in working with open access materials, the nature of the course modifications proposed, and any challenges or barriers anticipated in carrying out plans
- At least one letter of support from the chair/director of the faculty member's unit

Completed applications were reviewed by a group of representatives from the library and LEC along with the associate provost for academic excellence. The application process opened in mid-November and remained open until early January, around the beginning of the spring semester.

Because the initial round of the initiative was conceived as a pilot project, the plan was to keep the initial group of awardees relatively small, ideally no more than five. Ultimately, the committee received three applications that met all of the conditions of the program and opted to fund those three. One proposal opted for the Modify tier, while the other two selected the Create tier and thus embarked on writing their own open textbooks. After notifying the faculty members whose proposals would be funded, the committee began developing the training series for the faculty members. Librarians assumed responsibility for providing training in two areas. First, the library's Copyright Taskforce developed and implemented a one-hour workshop that covered copyright basics, particularly with regard to rules that faculty need to know when creating open textbooks. The workshop outlined appropriate guidelines for reusing a variety of material types so that the open textbook authors understood what they could and could not do based on U.S. copyright law and fair use. For example, faculty members were taught how to embed links to library resources that redirected through the library's proxy server, so the students using the book could access those resources using their university credentials. In addition, each recipient was partnered with a research librarian who was tasked with helping the author identify library resources or openly available materials that were appropriate for inclusion within the textbook. Each faculty member met at least once with their designated librarian, but at least one participant scheduled ongoing meetings with her librarian to continue working on the textbook. LEC staff assumed responsibility for the remaining two training opportunities. They worked with the authors to provide training in instructional technology needs that the authors encountered while building the books. For this, the LEC staff asked the recipients to identify the areas where they wanted additional training and then developed a customized training session for each participant. The LEC also worked with the associate provost for academic excellence to pair each author with a faculty mentor who could offer guidance in instructional pedagogy, particularly regarding strategies for deciding what types of content the books should cover and ideas for integrating the books into the course.

Upon completing the training sessions, faculty set out on the process of creating or compiling their open textbooks. Some chose to take a more collaborative approach, continuing to work closely with their assigned librarian and faculty mentor, while others worked more independently. Faculty members completed their textbooks over the course of the spring and summer semesters in 2016, and the completed books were utilized for the first time during the fall 2016 semester. At the completion of the fall semester, the committee evaluated the program along three criteria. The amount of savings generated was calculated based on the number of students enrolled in the course and the cost of the traditional textbook that was replaced by the open textbook. Overall student performance in the courses was compared to that of previous semesters to see if there is any demonstrable difference. Finally, both the faculty participants and their students were surveyed in an effort to get a sense of their experiences and opinions of the effectiveness of the open textbook. These findings were then used to identify ways to improve the initiative the next year.

LESSONS LEARNED

Now that the first round of the Open Textbook Initiative is complete, there are several important lessons learned along the way that will be vital to the success of the subsequent rounds of the program. For instance, now that everyone involved with the program has a sense of the amount of time needed to develop the textbooks, future participants will have a more structured time line. This will help the faculty members to have a sense of the amount of time they need to be prepared to devote to the project, and will also provide librarians with an opportunity to provide additional support to a recipient if it becomes apparent that one of the recipients is having trouble meeting the benchmarks. In addition, the application process will start earlier next year, thereby giving awardees a chance to start on the process of building the books earlier in the year.

Several new ideas for promoting the program are being considered. During the month of October, the library will host three events to promote OERs and the Open Textbook Initiative. The first session will offer an overview of OERs, including a discussion of their benefits for both faculty and students. The next event will provide suggestions on finding materials that can be included in an open textbook. In essence, this session will be like the one-on-one sessions that librarians provided for the first-year recipients, only in workshop form for a larger audience. The last session will be a panel discussion that will include participants from the initial round of the Open Textbook Initiative to share their experiences in both creating and using the textbooks. These presentations will lead into the call for applications for the second round of the initiative, which hopes to fund as many as ten proposals this round, potentially as much as $16,000 in grant funding if ten Create proposals are accepted. Once again, the Provost's Office and the libraries will each provide 50 percent of the funding needed for the grants.

Another key outreach goal of the initiative going forward is increasing student involvement in the push for open textbooks. During the first round, students expressed concern about textbook costs but did not have enough familiarity with open textbooks to make a strong advocacy case for their adoption. However, the newly elected president of the campus Student Government Association (SGA) specifically included addressing textbook costs as a goal of her presidential platform. This gives the library an excellent opportunity to use the first round of the Open Textbook Initiative as a springboard for a partnership with the SGA to get students involved in leading the call for more open textbooks on campus. In light of the successes of the initial pilot of the initiative, the broader connections between the program and other campus goals, and the opportunities to grow the program going forward, there is tremendous potential through this initiative for open textbooks to become a substantial part of the campus culture in the years to come.

CONCLUSION

There are still many barriers to introducing open textbooks on many campuses. Because of their expertise, librarians are well positioned to take on the challenge of explaining the value of open textbooks to faculty, students, and administrators. Thus, it is essential that librarians take the lead in demonstrating to their campus community the ways in which open textbooks align with other campus goals and initiatives. By doing so, these librarians not only have a better chance of securing buy-in for an open textbook program, but they also demonstrate another area in which the library brings significant value to the campus.

Notes

1. For a full overview of Mississippi's new IHL funding policy, see "Performance Allocation Model Summary," Mississippi Institutes of Higher Learning, last modified April 18, 2013, www.mississippi.edu/downloads/ihl_130418-2.pdf.
2. Much has been written elsewhere about the burden of textbook costs for students, but a helpful overview is available from the Student PIRGs website at http://studentpirgs.org/campaigns/sp/make-textbooks-affordable.
3. University of Southern Mississippi, Office of Institutional Research, "Common Data Set 2015–2016," 18–19, https://www.usm.edu/sites/default/files/groups/office-institutional-research/pdf/cds_2015-2016.pdf.
4. Rick Anderson, *Libraries, Leadership, and Scholarly Communication* (Chicago: American Library Association, 2016), 5.
5. Anderson, *Libraries, Leadership*, 5–6; Greg Seymour and Ann Connolly, "The Modern Repository: Aligning the Library with the University Mission" (presentation, University of Southern Mississippi, Hattiesburg, MS, April 29, 2016).
6. The university's Textbook and Course Materials Advisory Committee is a standing committee consisting of a faculty representative from each academic college and from the Gulf Coast Campus, as well as ex officio representatives from the campus bookstore, Institutional Research, Office of Disability Accommodations, Office of the Registrar, and University Libraries. The committee serves in an advisory role to the Office of the Provost on policies and procedures for ordering and implementing textbooks on campus.
7. More information about the Open Education Initiative at UMass Amherst can be found at https://www.library.umass.edu/services/teaching-and-learning/oer/open-education-initiative/.
8. Marilyn S. Billings, "The Open Education Initiative at UMass Amherst: Seeking Alternatives to High-Cost Textbooks" (presentation, University of Southern Mississippi, Hattiesburg, MS, April 17, 2015).

Bibliography

Anderson, Rick. *Libraries, Leadership, and Scholarly Communication.* Chicago: American Library Association, 2016.

Billings, Marilyn S. "The Open Education Initiative at UMass Amherst: Seeking Alternatives to High-Cost Textbooks." Presentation, University of Southern Mississippi, Hattiesburg, MS, April 17, 2015.

"Performance Allocation Model Summary." Mississippi Institutes of Higher Learning, last modified April 18, 2013. www.mississippi.edu/downloads/ihl_130418–2.pdf.

Seymour, Greg, and Ann Connolly, "The Modern Repository: Aligning the Library with the University Mission." Presentation, University of Southern Mississippi, Hattiesburg, MS, April 29, 2016.

University of Southern Mississippi, Office of Institutional Research. "Common Data Set 2015–2016," 18–19. https://www.usm.edu/sites/default/files/groups/office-institutional -research/pdf/cds_2015-2016.pdf.

DISRUPTING THE MODEL
Fostering Cultural Change through Academic Partnerships

Aimee deNoyelles, John Raible, Penny Beile, and Sarah Norris

The escalating cost of a higher education in the United States is receiving increased attention. The rising cost of college textbooks and course materials is one factor contributing to this. The U.S. Government Accountability Office reported that textbook prices have increased 82 percent from 2002 to 2012, while overall consumer inflation rose 27 percent.[1] On average, students spend around $1,300 per year on course materials at public four-year institutions.[2] The amount that students spend on course materials has recently declined, in part because the inflated expense drives students to sometimes avoid purchasing textbooks altogether.[3] While college affordability is a systemic issue, faculty, librarians, and instructional designers can make an impact by transitioning traditional course materials to lower-cost options.

Recent federal and state laws have been passed to promote more affordable course materials. At the national level, Section 133 of the Higher Education Opportunity Act of 2008 contains language to ensure that "students have access to affordable course materials by decreasing costs to students and enhancing transparency and disclosure with respect to the selection, purchase, sale, and use of course materials."[4] The Affordable College Textbook Bill was introduced to Congress in 2015, seeking to provide federal support to create and maintain open higher education textbooks.[5] Several states have responded accordingly. For example, in 2008 Florida passed statute 1004.085, the Textbook Affordability Act.[6] This was in response to the Board of Governors' charge for each institution to establish "textbook adoption procedures to minimize the cost of textbooks for students while maintaining the quality of education and academic freedom."[7] The statute was revised in 2016. Major changes included critically scrutinizing new textbook editions, creating and using open educational resources such as open textbooks, and institutional reporting of textbook adoption and prices of general education textbooks.[8]

These laws broadly impact colleges and universities in the United States; however, at the University of Central Florida (UCF), there are no institution-level initiatives or dedicated personnel to directly address textbook affordability at the time of this writing. In this quickly changing climate, several librarians and instructional designers at UCF have formed a unique partnership in the form of a working group to foster change regarding the affordability of course materials. The purpose of this chapter is to characterize the cultural environment in which the group operates, describe the nature of the group, and explain the collective efforts to make change from the top down and bottom up. In the conclusion, the working group model is presented, along with recommendations and reflection on future directions.

CULTURAL ENVIRONMENT

Organizational Structure

It is first necessary to describe the overall organizational structure at the university, and explain where the working group members reside (see figure 8.1). There are two major tiers of leadership at the institution: the President's Office and the Provost's Office. The President's Office oversees the nonacademic areas of the institution: General Counsel, Administration and Finance, and Business Services, which is the primary university liaison to the campus bookstore. The Provost's Office is responsible for the academic areas: the teaching and learning division, the UCF Libraries, and the Center for Distributed

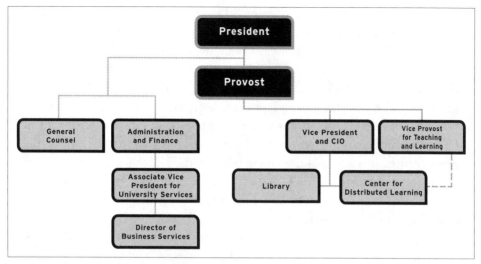

Figure 8.1 | **Textbook Affordability Stakeholders**

Learning (CDL). The libraries support teaching, learning, and research by providing information resources, services, facilities, and technology. A subject librarian model, in which each academic program has a dedicated librarian, was implemented in 2013. The CDL serves as the central agent for online learning at UCF, providing leadership in distance learning policies, strategies, and practices. Similar to the subject librarian model, instructional designers collaborate with instructors in certain departments to consult and support. The libraries and CDL are located in the same division (represented in figure 8.1 as falling under the vice-president and CIO for instructional technology and resources) and have similar academic support roles, thus leading to a sensible collaborative effort. Figure 8.1 showcases the many stakeholders who directly and indirectly influence textbook affordability issues, and also demonstrates the inherent conflict between the educational, nonprofit mission and financial center of the university. With regard to textbook affordability efforts on campus, the most visible example of this tension is the potential to disrupt the revenue stream supplied by the bookstore.

Catalysts

Prior to forming the partnership, both the libraries and the CDL had undertaken separate efforts to bring the textbook affordability discussion to the attention of faculty and students. In 2012, the vice president of the CDL called for members of the Instructional Design team to identify key players, understand what options were available, and grasp how instructors and students could potentially benefit from the use of digital textbooks. A few instructional designers took action in several ways: the forming of a special interest group; deployment of a survey to UCF students and faculty about digital textbook practices; and various demonstrations of reading technologies and devices. Conversations began with an e-textbook company to provide e-textbooks directly in UCF's learning management system. In order for integration to take place, the group learned that a formal agreement between the university and the provider was required. The University Office of General Counsel determined that the agreement violated the institution's contractual agreement with the bookstore provider, which states that the provider is the "exclusive University-owned property buyer and seller of all required, recommended or suggested course materials and tools, including books and course packs, including any of these materials which are published or distributed electronically, or sold over the Internet through any links associated with the University of Central Florida."[9] This response led two coauthors to take a focused look at this contract and compare it to others in the state university system. The comparative analysis revealed that the majority of the Florida bookstore contracts were exclusive sellers, although some had more flexibility concerning textbook affordability measures. This analysis provided a more informed understanding of the local and state landscape, and how UCF's contract with the bookstore provider could be modified to better support textbook affordability efforts.

The exclusivity clause in the bookstore contract has also affected library efforts. In 2014 a textbook affordability research guide that offered alternative ways to obtain textbooks was created, but after it came to the attention of university administrators the guide was asked to be removed due to the "exclusive campus bookseller provision" language in the bookstore contract.[10] Armed with federal and state legislative mandates, such as the Higher Education Opportunity Act and a 2008 state statute, the librarian who created the guide and the associate director of the libraries met with attorneys from the Office of General Counsel. After discussion, the librarians were stunned by counsel's conclusion that existing textbook affordability legislation was not written strongly enough to override the exclusivity clause of the bookstore contract. Of most concern was a link to a searchable third-party database that compared the cost of textbooks across Amazon, Chegg, the bookstore provider, and other vendors. Counsel maintained that they "did not have a dog in this fight," and their decision was based solely on the lack of direct language in the legislation to address the cost of course materials. Consequently, the guide was removed. On the positive side, counsel did maintain that the use of free, open course materials and library-sourced materials was not in conflict with the exclusivity clause.

Aside from discussions about textbook affordability at several library faculty meetings and a presentation by Springer publishing representatives, librarian efforts languished until a new academic program was approved. In 2015 the College of Business Administration introduced its new integrated business program. Seeking a competitive edge by lowering the cost of the degree, eight core courses were specifically developed for the new major with the provision that all classes would make use of open, current resources rather than rely solely on textbooks. Several librarians commented that they were working with their respective business faculty to locate high-quality course materials that were free to students, and went on to add that they also had been in contact with instructional designers, who were likewise supporting faculty with new course development. An informal working group of librarians and instructional designers began meeting regularly to discuss issues, suggest course content to academic faculty, and identify course materials for the eight courses. As that project concluded, the group discussed prior efforts to support textbook affordability and realized that we had many of the same goals and perceived barriers. A partnership was born, and the group began meeting regularly.

Nature of Collaborative Efforts

Currently, the core working group consists of three librarians and two instructional designers, and is complemented by other librarians and instructional designers who join on an "as-warranted" basis to support program faculty in transitioning to free, library-sourced or low-cost alternatives to traditional textbooks. Over time, the working group articulated a mission, identified immediate and long-term goals, shared knowledge, solicited faculty participation, and communicated intent and progress to key university stakeholders. The efforts of the group can be classified in two broad ways: macro and micro. The goal of the macro, "top-down" approach is to positively influence the large-scale factors that affect change at the university level, and an example is meeting with campus leaders and advocating for policy change concerning course materials exclusivity and booklist ownership. The micro, "bottom-up" grassroots approach to promoting textbook affordability includes marketing to individual faculty in various ways, including campus presentations, facilitating the efforts of those interested in migrating course materials, and conducting research with program faculty.

Macro Efforts

One objective of the working group was to inform UCF leadership about local, state, and national textbook affordability efforts. Almost immediately upon forming, high-level administrators were invited to discuss college affordability legislative mandates, the group's goals, and the perceived barriers concerning the bookstore contract. Representatives from Business Services (which oversees the contract), General Counsel, Student Accessibility Services, administrative units charged with complying with textbook legislative mandates, and vice-presidents and vice-provosts with an interest in the topic attended the meeting. The results of the contract analysis were presented, and specific language that would be more favorable to textbook affordability adoption at the institution was proposed. General Counsel reiterated their opinion that open or library-sourced materials were not in competition with the bookstore contract, which provided an avenue in which to begin our work.

Another macro-level effort is gaining access to the university's required textbook list, in order to further pursue low-cost or open materials. The main challenge appeared in the language in the existing bookstore contract, which states, "[bookstore provider] creates a computer database containing, among other things, course book adoption information. These forms and the database are [bookstore provider] proprietary information."[11] Without access to the textbook list, we could not easily identify required course materials already licensed by the library or available openly online. Another campus unit, Student Accessibility Services, likewise was interested in accessing the booklist. After attending a meeting of high-level campus administrators and regional bookstore managers to discuss access to the booklist, both interested parties were able to secure the list after submitting a Higher Education Opportunity Act (HEOA) request. At the current time, we are working with library Acquisitions to run the 12,500 titles against library holdings.

We continue to reach out to and work with pertinent campus units, and have formed a relationship with the Faculty Center for Teaching and Learning (and have presented on the topic twice at their faculty development institutes). We also continue to meet with Business Services regarding the upcoming bookstore contract renewal, and members met with consultants writing criteria for the new bookstore contract, which is being renegotiated in 2017. Thanks to the group input, more inclusive language was presented to honor textbook affordability measures. A quarterly update is sent to each of the units regarding our successes and activities.

Micro Efforts

We also have facilitated individual faculty efforts to transition to free or lower-cost course materials. The expectation is that these efforts will prove successful, word will spread, and whole departments will begin adopting cost-saving course materials.

Presentations at faculty development conferences within the institution have proven effective in recruiting faculty interested in migrating to free or low-cost course materials. The authors also gave a presentation about the open textbook provider OpenStax and invited librarians, instructional designers, interested faculty, and campus administrators to attend. We found that despite the lack of monetary incentives, faculty attend the presentations and are interested in textbook affordability because they desire a competitive edge concerning student enrollment. All share the belief that costs are simply too high.

Several projects have been undertaken at the individual faculty level. From these efforts, three approaches organically emerged: (1) locate open-licensed or copyright-free versions of existing course materials; (2) offer open alternatives to the traditional textbook; and (3) replace an existing textbook with an OER. In this section, three case studies will be presented. Each example includes a description of the project, the roles and resources involved, projected savings to students, and an evaluation. Projected cost savings of the three examples are presented later in the chapter (see figure 8.3 on page 114).

<hr>

Case #1
Locate open-licensed or copyright-free
versions of existing course materials

During spring 2016, the UCF Libraries subject librarian for English contacted an English literature lecturer regarding open alternatives to the course-required text. The early English literature textbook was comprised of readings from the medieval period through the late eighteenth century, with much of the content available in the public domain. The course typically experiences enrollments of 75–80 students during the fall and spring semesters and 35–40 students during the summer semester. The lecturer was interested in finding out more information in regard to a possible open solution to the required textbook.

With the required reading list in hand, the libraries' Office of Scholarly Communication worked in conjunction with the English subject librarian to conduct an analysis of the required reading list, looking for freely accessible and acceptable public domain versions of each text on the list. The Scholarly Communication adjunct created a spreadsheet of all required texts with open alternative options, which the English subject librarian, Scholarly Communication librarian, and the lecturer were able to review for appropriateness and copyright compliance.

After completing the analysis, the working group and the English subject librarian met with the lecturer to discuss options for providing open alternative texts for the course. Of the texts analyzed for the course, only a small number had particular copyright-related issues, including several with translations. It was determined that one text would be translated by the lecturer, who applied a Creative Commons license to this translation, in an effort to provide an accessible version to others outside of the institution. Additionally, the group was unable to obtain an open version of a specific text translation. The lecturer decided that this reading would be the only text to be purchased by the students in the course since it was available at a nominal fee. Despite having to purchase the one text, the students saw a significant savings.

Once open readings were identified, an instructional designer in the working group created an EPUB version of the readings using an open source software called Sigil. This was done to provide a uniform reading experience for students, because source readings were found in their original versions in various file formats and quality levels. This proved to be the most laborious part of the process, as the formatting and re-versioning of text into the EPUB format was both time-consuming and challenging. During this time, several additional questions regarding copyright arose, in particular Creative Commons licenses and permissions from the original copyright holders. In addition to formatting and copyright considerations, proper attributions were added to the required text.

A survey was distributed at the end of the summer 2016 course to gather information about students' perceptions of these open, digital readings. Eighteen of the 22 students who responded to the question indicated that they accessed the readings that were located in each module, and 3 primarily used the e-book version. Nineteen of the 22 found the digital readings easy to access and use, while 17 indicated that the EPUB was easy to read and study from. The only concern was one comment about file sizes and pages loading slowly. Perhaps most rewarding was one student's summary: "Most importantly, the fact that the textbook was free is probably the best benefit. However, there are many more benefits from using the online textbook. It was much easier to be able to take the book anywhere, whether it be on a phone, laptop, tablet, etc. Also, if you're like me, and you like to physically hold paper and write notes out, you could easily print out the PDF pages and have a hard copy in your hands. Overall, I think that the online textbook is a FANTASTIC idea."

Case #2
Offering open alternatives
to the traditional textbook

While researching high-quality open online textbooks, an instructional designer discovered OpenStax, a grant-funded open textbook initiative hosted by Rice University. After contacting OpenStax and receiving a list of UCF faculty who were utilizing their materials, she found that one was a microeconomics professor from the College of Business Administration. The popular introductory course enrolls approximately 1,400 students in a single course section and is offered as a "lecture-capture" format, where students can come to the live class session, watch the session streamed online, or watch the recording online later. While the professor lists a "traditional" textbook on his syllabus (which costs around $200 for a new edition), he also mentions that the OpenStax book could be used as a free alternative.

Intrigued by the idea of offering an open textbook as an alternative, working group members proposed to conduct research in the spring 2016 and summer 2016 sections of the course by surveying students to find out which book(s) they reviewed and used, and their perceptions of the reading experience. Out of a total of 1,568 students, 123 completed the survey, resulting in an 8 percent response rate. The results are preliminary since the participation rate was low, but some unexpected findings were revealed. First, nearly half of all participants chose to forgo using either textbook because they indicated that the lectures were sufficient enough to be successful in the course. Second, 80 percent of the participants who used the open textbook said that they primarily chose it because it was affordable. As one student noted, "The fact that I could use an alternative book for free was the deciding factor and truly the only factor I used when selecting a book for this class." Another declared, "It was a great alternative to buying the book. I usually prefer hard copies of textbooks, but I was okay with using this one because it didn't cost me a penny." Finally, and perhaps most importantly, participants using the open textbook agreed or

THE TEXTBOOK I PRIMARILY USED FOR THIS COURSE WAS:	OFFICIAL BOOK (*n* = 35)		OPENSTAX (*n* = 19)	
	n	%	*n*	%
Easy to acquire	31	88.57	19	100.00
Easy to use	23	65.71	18	94.74
Easy to read	23	65.71	18	94.74
Easy to study from	18	51.43	16	84.21
High in quality	24	68.57	18	94.74
Credible	29	82.86	18	94.74
Valuable	20	57.14	19	100.00
Relevant to course	19	54.29	19	100.00
Supported performance	19	54.29	15	78.95
Prepared me for exams	18	51.43	12	63.16
Increased interest	7	20.00	7	36.84
Increased learning	19	54.29	14	73.68
Increased enjoyment	8	22.86	6	31.58
Encouraged me to think about course content in a new way	10	28.57	6	31.58
Challenged the way I think	14	40.00	7	36.84

Figure 8.2 | **Microeconomics Student Survey Results—
Spring and Summer 2016**

strongly agreed at a higher rate than students who used the "official" course text in response to questions about the ease of use and quality of the open textbooks (see figure 8.2).

Students who used the OpenStax textbook rated their reading experience higher than students who used the traditional textbook on every survey item except for "the textbook challenged the way I think" (although the difference is slight). These results suggest that the open textbook was perceived as high in quality and served as a more than suitable alternative to the costly textbook. Conducting this research allowed us to make recommendations to the instructor, namely, offering the print version of the OpenStax book in the bookstore for rental/purchase, being more clear about the open option in the syllabus, and tailoring the content more to the OpenStax book (or at least indicating which weekly reading goes with which chapter in the text).

Case #3
Replace existing textbook with an OER

In the spring of 2016, we were approached by an American history lecturer who had attended a campus presentation we had previously given. The faculty member was interested in a low-cost alternative to the current costly textbook. We recommended using an OpenStax textbook, and instructional designers on the project secured a print version of the text from OpenStax for his review. The instructional designers also secured and reviewed the digital companion components, such as presentation slides and test questions, and formatted and uploaded quiz questions into the faculty member's online course. As this was a new model, the bookstore was consulted to determine the "proper" way to make the print version available at the cheapest possible price (in this case, through rental options).

A survey was distributed in the faculty member's summer 2016 course, and the results were positive. Twelve of the thirteen students who responded to the survey used the digital version of the textbook and found it easy to acquire. They also found it valuable and relevant to the course, and felt the open text supported their course performance. Eleven of thirteen indicated that the digital textbook was high in quality, easy to use, increased their learning, and prompted them to think about the course content in a new way. Ten of thirteen respondents found the resource easy to read and study from, and felt that the text helped prepare them for tests. The concerns of the faculty member about using a digital text were largely alleviated, and based on student perceptions and performance, the faculty member used the OpenStax text for a larger number in the fall and spring. In a recent meeting, the faculty member noted that his course was no longer a required general education class and that marketing his course as a no-cost textbook could result in a competitive advantage over other classes that require expensive texts.

Potential cost savings for students for each of the three case study examples follow (see figure 8.3). The savings are based on cost of the traditional text, current cost (if any), and average number of enrollments by year. Savings are projected for one and five years.

SUBJECT	POTENTIAL SAVINGS ($): 1 SEMESTER	PROJECTED SAVINGS ($): 1 YEAR	PROJECTED SAVINGS ($): 5 YEARS
English	2,660	13,300	66,000
Microeconomics	285,800	700,000	3,500,000
History	1,840	28,160	140,800

Figure 8.3 | **Projected Savings from Current Projects**

CONCLUSION

This chapter described the genesis and nature of a working group that organically formed to address textbook affordability on a large university campus in the absence of institutionally led textbook affordability initiatives. Over time, as goals and projects evolved, our workflow and processes also developed organically. As figure 8.2 indicates, much of the grassroots activity is driven by the instructional designer's and subject librarian's relationships with program faculty. As librarians and instructional designers, working group members both reach out to faculty and help support others with textbook affordability adoption projects. The workflow continues by meeting with faculty and discussing objectives, and then the librarian and/or instructional designer looks for open, library-sourced, or low-cost course material. The review of copyright permissions of material is performed by the Scholarly Communication librarian. Upon faculty approval, materials are created and integrated into the course; this step is accomplished primarily by the instructional designers. Evaluation of the product and revision are critical final steps performed by the working group in conjunction with the faculty member. This workflow resulted from three scenarios: (1) existing open-licensed materials are adopted as is; (2) the working group comes together to find and adopt existing resources, dealing with issues such as copyright and licensing, as well as technical production; and (3) a new product is created by faculty and the working group, and openly licensed. This model is one that could be replicated at other institutions. (See figure 8.4.)

Several important factors—namely, scalability, collaboration, and evaluation—have been identified that could prove useful to others in similar situations. Ultimately, the process of working with individual faculty, as it currently exists, is neither feasible nor scalable without additional staff resources. For instance, transitioning the English literature textbook to a compilation of open

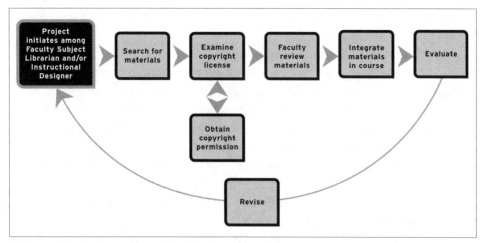

Figure 8.4 | **Working Group Workflow and Process**

or library-sourced readings was time- and labor-intensive and would be difficult to "scale up" to the institutional level. The value of collaboration also emerged as a theme of successful projects. The core working group members continue to be instructional designers and librarians, but representatives from Student Accessibility Services, Business Services, the division of teaching and learning, and compliance officers all have a stake and vested interest in what we are doing. Communication is an underlying motif of each recommendation, and is the cornerstone of successful collaboration. Finally, evaluations are necessary to show the effectiveness and outcomes of this process. Not only were survey results shared with faculty, but also with institutional stakeholders. Certainly, reports that 71 percent of the survey participants decided not to purchase a textbook because of high cost, and 81 percent delayed the purchase (at least once in their college careers) are cause for discussion at the institutional level.

From our initial work, a number of goals we established are coming to fruition while others continue to be added. We have decided to continue to work with individual faculty who want to transition to free or lower-cost course materials, but we realize that the largest return on investment will be locating one-to-one replacements with library-sourced e-books and articles and working with General Education Program coordinators to adopt open textbooks in lieu of traditional ones. Now that the textbook list has been acquired, it is being run against library holdings to identify library-sourced materials. Program instructors will be contacted about the potential to replace the existing textbook with one supplied by the library. Further research on classroom practices and textbook affordability projects also will be conducted. Assessment of the student experience is key to getting faculty buy-in and bringing textbook affordability issues to the forefront of the institution.

On a macro level, we will continue exploring the impact of the recently passed state legislation on the existing bookstore contract. Success here will allow us the option to pilot and possibly implement an OER/low-cost alternative platform, establish a presence about textbook affordability on the university website, and work with relevant campus units to explore additional, large-scale cost-saving measures. One outcome of our relationship with institutional stakeholders was the opportunity to provide input into the renegotiation of the bookstore contract. In addition, we have been able to secure some modest funding in partnership with the Faculty Center for Teaching and Learning in order for several faculty to discover, review, create, and share open educational resources in 2017.

The question remains, did we disrupt the model and foster cultural change? Although too soon to give an unequivocal "yes," we are disrupting the model through our talks with campus administrators and our work with individual faculty. Did we foster cultural change through partnerships? Certainly, the academic conversation is changing here. However, for real cultural change to take place, a few things still need to happen: (1) act upon the library holdings of course materials identified from acquiring the textbook list; (2) increase the use of open course materials in general education courses that reach thousands of students, which is dependent upon getting support from program coordinators as well as individual faculty; and (3) further expand relationships with campus units. Creating cultural change requires cultural buy-in. For us, the heart of this effort is working with faculty in creating and sharing open and low-cost course materials. This will take time, expertise, and support. We have demonstrated that we can successfully lower the cost of a college education and our work to date stands as proof of that concept. However, an official charge and/or staff or financial support would make this a reality quicker. And another goal is added to the list.

Notes

1. U.S. Government Accountability Office, *College Textbooks: Students Have Greater Access to Textbook Information*, GAO-13–368 (Washington, DC, 2013), 17, www.gao.gov/products/GAO-13–368.

2. "Tuition and Fees by Sector and State over Time," College Board, http://trends.collegeboard.org/college-pricing/figures-tables/tuition-fees-sector-state-over-time.

3. Jeffrey R. Young, "In Students' Minds, Textbooks Are Increasingly Optional Purchases," *The Chronicle of Higher Education*, 2015, http://chronicle.com/article/in-students-minds -textbooks/231455.

4. Higher Education Opportunity Act, U.S. Code 1001 (2008), §§ 133 et seq.

5. "The Affordable College Textbook Act," Scholarly Publishing and Academic Resources Coalition, http://sparcopen.org/our-work/2016-act-bill/.

6. Textbook Affordability, § 1004.085, Fla. Stat. (2008).

7. Textbook and Instructional Materials Affordability, § 1004.085, Fla. Stat. (2016).

8. Textbook Adoption, Fla. Bd. Govs. R. 8.003 (2008).

9. "Agreement for Bookstore Management and Related Services between the University of Central Florida Board of Trustees and Barnes & Noble College Bookstores, Inc.," University of Central Florida, https://purchasing.ucf.edu/wp-content/uploads/ sites/3/2016/05/Barnes-Nobles_Contract-.pdf.

10. Ibid.

11. Ibid.

Bibliography

"The Affordable College Textbook Act." Scholarly Publishing and Academic Resources Coalition. http://sparcopen.org/our-work/2016-act-bill/.

"Agreement for Bookstore Management and Related Services between the University of Central Florida Board of Trustees and Barnes & Noble College Bookstores, Inc." University of Central Florida. https://purchasing.ucf.edu/wp-content/uploads/ sites/3/2016/05/Barnes-Nobles_Contract-.pdf.

Higher Education Opportunity Act. U.S. Code 1001 (2008), §§ 133 et seq.

Textbook Adoption. Fla. Bd. Govs. R. 8.003 (2008).

Textbook and Instructional Materials Affordability. § 1004.085, Fla. Stat. (2016).

"Tuition and Fees by Sector and State over Time." College Board. http://trends.collegeboard .org/college-pricing/figures-tables/tuition-fees-sector-state-over-time.

U.S. Government Accountability Office. *College Textbooks: Students Have Greater Access to Textbook Information*, GAO-13–368, 17. Washington, DC, 2013. www.gao.gov/ products/GAO-13–368.

Young, Jeffrey R. "In Students' Minds, Textbooks Are Increasingly Optional Purchases." *The Chronicle of Higher Education*. 2015. http://chronicle.com/article/in-students -minds-textbooks/231455.

TEXTBOOK AND OER PRACTICES IN THE HUMANITIES AND SOCIAL SCIENCES

A Case Study at the University of Florida

April Hines, Stacey Ewing, Colleen Seale, and Melissa Clapp

I n summer 2015, the Florida Association of College and Research Libraries (FACRL) revealed the theme of their upcoming fall program, "Tackling the Textbook Problem: Leveraging Library Resources and OERs to Reduce Costs." The program's focus was in reaction to the growing textbook affordability problem, not only in the state of Florida, but across the nation. A 2014 study conducted by the U.S. Public Interest Research Group revealed that "textbook costs have grown by 82% during the last 10 years—three times the rate of inflation."[1] On the state level, in a 2012 survey conducted by the Florida Virtual Campus, 64 percent of college students reported not purchasing a required textbook due to high costs, negatively affecting class selection and educational outcomes.[2] At the University of Florida (UF), undergraduates are spending approximately $1,200 per year on course materials, according to the UF Office for Student Financial Affairs.[3] In response, a team of humanities and social sciences (HSS) librarians at UF decided to examine the use of textbooks, open educational resources, and library curriculum support in the

HSS departments they serve. Were faculty in the humanities and social sciences primarily using traditional textbooks, or had they started to utilize alternative resources in an effort to reduce student debt? To what extent were OERs and open access materials being used in the classroom, and how were librarians and library resources helping to replace costly course materials? In this chapter, the authors present an analysis of 200 course syllabi from 25 HSS disciplines and describe future outreach and marketing strategies to promote library resources and OER options in order to tackle the textbook affordability problem.

LITERATURE REVIEW: TEXTBOOK AFFORDABILITY IN FLORIDA

At the national level, there is a robust and growing body of literature on textbook affordability and the development of alternative resources. In the state of Florida, the legislature has been involved in several efforts to provide open educational resources for well over a decade and continues to examine how to assist students with more affordable textbook options and support OERs. An early and ongoing effort, the Orange Grove, was established in 2004 as a digital repository of freely available, K-20 educational resources as well as a platform for schools, colleges, and universities to incorporate OERs into their course offerings. The repository includes learning objects, open access textbooks, courseware, 3D object models, and videos. Currently, there are a limited number of textbooks in this repository that fall under the humanities and/or social sciences category. In 2008, to further support provisions of the federal Higher Education Opportunity Act, the Florida Legislature passed legislation to promote open access textbooks in an effort to help reduce student textbook costs (Florida Statute 1004.085 Textbook Affordability). In 2009 the Florida Department of Education charged a Textbook Affordability Workgroup to make recommendations on textbook availability.

In 2010, 2012, and most recently in 2016, three statewide surveys were conducted by the Florida Distance Learning Consortium and the Florida Virtual Campus to further assess student textbook acquisition and usage. Key findings from the 2012 report, with 22,000 respondents, indicated that students were generally unaware of open textbooks and open courseware, but would be willing to pay a small textbook materials fee for each course that uses an open textbook. Forty-four percent of the student respondents were aware that the libraries provided some textbooks for checkout; however, 47 percent did not know about this service.[4]

Additional legislation was passed on April 14, 2016, when Florida Governor Rick Scott signed House Bill 7019: Education Access and Affordability into law. According to the Florida Department of Education, the law expands textbook affordability provisions to include instructional materials, promotes public awareness concerning the cost of higher education, and further specifies the responsibilities of Florida colleges and universities in relation to textbook affordability.[5]

Some library-related efforts around the state include the Textbook Affordability Project (TAP) established by the University of South Florida (USF) and the USF Tampa Library in 2010. Rollins College Library has established an OER Grant Program to encourage faculty to develop and use OERs for their courses. At UF, a current project, Orange Grove Texts *Plus*, addresses the local issue of OERs. Orange Grove Texts *Plus* is the open access imprint of the University of Florida Press and is a joint initiative with the UF Libraries. The project is still in the early stages and it is too soon to determine its impact on OER use in the humanities and social sciences at UF.

METHODOLOGY AND DATA

The project team of HSS librarians at the University of Florida examined syllabi from 3000-level classes offered during the spring semester of 2015. All syllabi were accessed from departmental websites per University of Florida open records policy, which requires that all course syllabi be posted online. Classes from the 3000-level were chosen because most undergraduate students are entering the core courses in their major at that level. Two hundred course syllabi from advertising, African American studies, anthropology, applied physiology and kinesiology, business, classics, criminology and law, economics, English, health education and behavior, history, journalism, languages, linguistics, literature and culture, mass communications, philosophy, political science, psychology, public relations, religion, sociology, telecommunication, theater, tourism, recreation and sport management, and women's studies were analyzed in this case study.

From the syllabi, we collected the following data: course title, course name, syllabus URL, textbook(s) required (yes/no), number of textbooks, additional readings (yes/no), number of additional readings, course pack(s) (yes/no), course reserves (yes/no), price of the book on Amazon.com, open access resource(s) (yes/no), held by the library (yes/no), library access noted on syllabus (yes/no), library links provided (yes/no), accurate library information (yes/no), and a notes field. It is worth noting that the data represent only what the project team found on the syllabi. Team members were unable to see additional content on eLearning platforms, course reserves pages, and/or course websites.

The findings were surprising. From the 200 syllabi, 167 classes (84 percent) required textbooks, while 33 (16 percent) did not. Figure 9.1 shows the courses with the most expensive textbook costs. Thirty-four classes (17 percent) used course reserves. Only 12 percent mentioned library access on their syllabi, with comments such as "*The Journal of Monetary Economics* can be downloaded for free from the libraries' website," and "Use library databases to access *The Economist* and *EIU Viewswire.*" Many of the courses utilizing course reserves only mentioned the name of the course reserve software, Ares, but did not mention the library by name at all. Some faculty provided step-by-step instructions for off-campus access or referenced a particular library collection (government documents), while others, unfortunately, listed outdated information about library resources and services (including listing a reading room that no longer

1. Intro to Information Systems	$390.00
2. Anthropology in Action	$298.00
3. Business Finance	$282.00
4. Cognitive Psychology	$255.00
5. Intermediate Microeconomics	$240.00
6. Healthcare Economics	$239.00
7. Introduction to Latin American Politics	$234.00
8. Sports Nutrition	$222.00
9. Social Psychology	$221.00
10. Comparative Psychology	$219.00
11. Financial Accounting and Reporting	$214.00
12. Intermediate Macroeconomics	$210.00
13. Applied Behavioral Analysis	$200.00

Figure 9.1 | **The Most Expensive Courses**

exists), clearly demonstrating a divide between teaching faculty and library staff. Figure 9.2 shows a sampling of instructor comments on syllabi pages.

Five percent still used course packs. In 113 of the classes (57 percent), the libraries own some of the materials listed in the syllabi. Twenty-three classes (12 percent) used freely available resources such as World Bank Open Data, Federal Reserve Bank of St. Louis economic data, public domain texts available through the Internet Archive, and a PBS miniseries on YouTube. To clarify, these "freely available resources" were not always open access. Twenty-eight classes (14 percent) indicated that additional readings were available via Canvas eLearning. No classes listed designated OERs on the syllabi.

The most expensive disciplines were as follows: psychology course materials had an average cost of $178.00, economics came in second with an average cost of $176.00, and business rounded out this group with $140.00 per class.

In general, the least expensive disciplines were English, mass communications, linguistics and languages, literatures, and cultures. Examples of the least expensive classes were Visual Journalism, $22.00; Business Chinese $41.00; Structure of Human Language $11.00; Modern English Structure $31.88; Pronunciation and TESL $25.00; Moral Philosophy $26.00; Politics in Russia $41.00; Introduction to Judaism $42.00; and Religion and Food $27.00.

Additionally, when speaking of OERs, the authors are referring to "free and openly licensed educational materials that can be used for teaching, learning and research."[6] Open access refers to resources that are "digital, free of charge, and free of copyright and licensing restrictions."[7] Furthermore, "openness,"

Faculty Quotes Taken from the Syllabi

"There are no suitable textbooks in this new field."

"You can get the articles online from the library, but doing that from off campus can be a challenge. I recommend you purchase the journal from the publisher."

"We will be using these books throughout the course, so you'll probably want to buy them."

"My advice for all majors is to purchase and learn to use the book as a resource."

Figure 9.2 | **Syllabi Quotes**

for the purpose of this study, also refers to materials that have no password requirements or are limited to students with identification cards.

Additional trends the authors found in syllabi include:

- Use of older editions.
- "Lost" library books—many of the previous editions of textbooks identified in the syllabi were designated "lost" in the library catalog.
- Modular course materials such as textbooks with supplementary online materials including multimedia components, quizzes, and assignments.
- Limited course pack usage.

SOLUTIONS FOR LEVERAGING LIBRARY MATERIALS AND OERS

The findings from the syllabi analysis revealed a great need for a targeted outreach and marketing plan that would assist subject specialists with connecting their faculty to resources and services that would ultimately reduce student textbook costs. Not a single instructor was using designated OERs in the classroom, and only 17 percent were making use of course reserves. Even more startling was the discovery that the library already owned content (in either electronic or print formats) for more than half of the classes analyzed, and yet only 12 percent of those courses even mentioned library access on the syllabus. In some cases, students were instructed to purchase articles from publications to which the library already subscribed, as well as titles available as e-books in the library catalog. There was an evident knowledge gap among faculty and numerous missed opportunities for librarians to assist in leveraging library resources to replace costly course materials.

In an effort to bridge the gap, the project team identified four key strategies that would comprise a marketing blueprint for student savings. The first strategy was designed to tackle the lack of library mentions on course syllabi. Many instructors at UF use a customizable syllabus template created by the Office of Faculty Development, which includes standard sections on academic honesty, the UF IT help desk, the Counseling and Wellness Center, and the university's honor code. Adding a simple library component to the template, with links to information on course reserves, research assistance, off-campus access, and interlibrary loan, could bring much-needed exposure to library resources and would require little effort from the instructor. A space could even be added for a link to the subject guide in a course's discipline, along with the name and contact information for their subject specialist.

In line with incorporating the library more prominently into course syllabi, a library presence in the university's course management system, Canvas, is equally as important. All instructors are provided with a basic course shell in Canvas with customizable tabs such as discussions, announcements, and modules. Conveniently, the UF Libraries' course reserve system, Ares, has the ability to integrate into Canvas with a simple "Course Reserves" tab, located prominently in the main menu. With one click, students can access library e-resources while working directly within their course content. There is also a "Commons" feature that allows instructors to upload modules, documents, videos, and so on and "share" with other Canvas users who can then "copy" the content to their own courses. Librarians may create generic documents or videos specific to the humanities and social sciences, giving users step-by-step instructions on how to locate and use library resources. These "modules" could then be easily selected and added to course sites based on instructor needs. The ease of use, tied directly to a platform that students and faculty use on a daily basis, eliminates many of the barriers to leveraging library resources in the classroom.

The third strategy arose from a concept that became apparent to the project team during the syllabi analysis: "Faculty are not going to come to us; we need to reach out to them." While instructors receive a standard, "Don't forget to submit course reserve requests" e-mail each semester, it was unclear if they understood all of the library services/resources available to them as they prepared course materials for a new semester. As a result, a more targeted, personal approach was devised wherein subject specialists would e-mail their faculty, offering to purchase multiuser-licensed e-book versions of class texts (when available), or help direct them to freely available or library-licensed materials in the form of journal articles, video tutorials, and so on that could potentially save their students money.

The team piloted this targeted approach and immediately heard back from several instructors, including a Law of Mass Communication professor whose $140 textbook was available for purchase as a multiuser e-book from the library's vendor. The cost for the library was $674 and saved over 200 students from having to purchase the book. This title is now the most used e-book in the UF Libraries' collection.

Another instructor worked with her librarian to link to journal articles and excerpts previously printed in a $30 course packet, and yet another was informed the library could purchase copyright permission to place chapter excerpts online—replacing an additional costly textbook. In a news reporting class moving to an online-only format, the instructor collaborated with his librarian to identify freely available video tutorials he could embed in his Canvas site in place of a traditional textbook. One subject specialist was even able to link his faculty to library-owned, streaming video content as an alternative to purchasing expensive DVDs with public viewing rights.

The project team discovered that faculty were more than willing to take advantage of library resources and services while drafting their course materials, but subject specialists had to initiate the process. For instance, one instructor, after being notified the library already owned her course textbook and would be happy to place it on course reserve, said, "That would be great! I want to be as helpful to cash-strapped students as possible."

Increasing the visibility of OERs among the UF community was the fourth strategy in the marketing plan. Subject specialists often found their patrons were simply unsure how to locate quality OERs in their subject area. A subject guide, created and maintained by UF's scholarly communications librarian, was identified as a key resource for promoting OERs to students and faculty. This guide includes a definition of OERs and their importance, in addition to links to top OER sites such as OER Commons, Merlot, and MITOpenCourseWare. Figure 9.3 shows a selection of OER resources. There are also resources further simplifying copyright guidelines for faculty, educating them on the kinds of materials they can reuse in the physical and virtual classroom.

Today there are many OER hosts that librarians can promote to faculty members	
BC Campus OpenEd	https://open.bccampus.ca
College Open Textbooks	http://collegeopentextbooks.org
MERLOT Open Textbook	https://www.merlot.org
OER Commons	https://www.oercommons.org
Openstax College	https://openstax.org/subjects
Open SUNY Textbooks	http://textbooks.opensuny.org
Open Textbook Library	http://open.umn.edu/opentextbooks
Saylor Academy	http://www.saylor.org/books
Textbook Equity	https://www.textbookequity.org

Figure 9.3 | **OER Options**

Subject specialists are also encouraged to identify and recommend high-quality, discipline-specific OERs to faculty for consideration. For example, the two most expensive disciplines found in the syllabi analysis were psychology and economics—with average textbook costs totaling more than $170 per class. Yet there are several peer-reviewed OER alternatives in these disciplines (written by top scholars) available for download from OpenStax .org, Rice University's OER initiative. How many faculty are simply unaware of these alternatives?

The project team also worked with the Cataloging and Discovery Services and e-Resources units to add OERs and open access materials to the library's catalog from the Directory of Open Access Books, the Open Textbook Library, Open SUNY Textbooks, and HathiTrust to enhance OER discoverability. ProQuest has also begun the process of adding OER metadata to Summon, our current discovery tool.

Moving forward, the project team has identified several long-term marketing and outreach strategies to promote leveraging library resources and OERs in the classroom.

These strategies include:

Offering financial incentives for faculty, in the form of internal library grant funding, to create OERs with the assistance of library staff such as Rollins College's OER Grant Program: www.rollins.edu/library/services/oer.html.

Further development of OrangeGrove Text *Plus*, a grant-funded, joint initiative between the University of Florida Press and the UF Libraries, where high-quality, out-of-print titles from the UF Press will be made available as digital books, hosted and made freely available by the UF Libraries. Providing access to such valuable academic resources will give faculty additional options when selecting no-cost course materials: www.ufdc.ufl.edu/ogt?n=ogtexts.

Organizing a student textbook swap or donation program on campus. Why sell or toss recent textbooks when students can help their peers?

Adopting more patron-driven acquisition (PDA) or evidence-based acquisition plans. Through regular automatic updates of recent scholarly materials in the library catalog, excluding titles from traditional textbook publishers such as Pearson, McGraw-Hill, and so on, more students can discover titles on course reading lists (i.e., Routledge handbooks, university press titles, etc.) and more faculty can identify materials to support their curriculum, thus initiating additional library purchases that will save students money.

Exploring the library's potential role in UF's future collaborative e-learning platform Unizin.org. Currently in development, Unizin is a digital teaching and learning environment founded by a consortium of universities, including the University of Florida, where faculty can quickly and easily upload and share their digital course content across institutions, using built-in open publishing tools. Increased access to such materials introduces faculty to alternative resources for replacing traditional textbooks.

Creating a textbook affordability fund, from which multiuser, e-book versions of required UF textbooks will automatically be purchased when available through library vendors.

Conducting additional assessment on textbook use and OER practices of UF faculty through surveys or by hosting focus groups. What are the potential barriers/concerns to using such materials in the classroom?

CONCLUSION

While the project team initiated the syllabi analysis to determine textbook use and OER practices in the academic departments they serve, the results indicated a much greater need for marketing and outreach of library services and resources. The findings showed that HSS faculty at the University of Florida are simply not including designated OERs in their course materials, and they rarely mention library access on syllabi, even when the library owns material for over half of the classes analyzed. Less than a quarter of courses in the study were utilizing course reserves and freely available resources, while the majority of classes were still requiring students to purchase traditional textbooks. These results fall in line with key findings from a national survey of over 3,000 faculty conducted by the Babson Survey Research Group, which found that only 5.3 percent of courses were using open textbooks, including public domain and Creative Commons licensed materials. The Babson Survey also found that the top barriers to adopting OERs for faculty were "there are not enough resources for my subject," it is "too hard to find what I need," and "there is no comprehensive catalog of resources."[8] These results present ample opportunities for librarians to play a role in assisting faculty with identifying quality OERs and open access resources to incorporate into their curricula, as well as to link instructors to library services and resources that can serve as alternatives to costly course materials. The project team identified four short-term outreach and marketing strategies and piloted a more personal, targeted approach in which subject specialists individually contacted faculty, offering to assist in saving their students money. We discovered that faculty were very open to this approach and were eager to take advantage of their librarian's proposals once offered. The project team also identified several long-term goals as a strategy for increasing the role of UF subject specialists in textbook affordability initiatives across campus, especially in the humanities and social sciences. The syllabi analysis revealed that librarians are in the perfect position to be the missing link in solving the growing textbook affordability problem as facilitators, subject specialists, and open access proponents. More effective marketing of the services and resources that libraries and librarians can offer will create a collaborative campus culture that ultimately results in saving students from spending thousands of dollars on costly course materials.

Notes

1. Ethan Senack, "Fixing the Broken Textbook Market: How Students Respond to High Textbook Costs and Demand Alternatives," U.S. PIRG Education Fund & the Student PIRGs, 2014, www.uspirg.org/sites/pirg/files/reports/NATIONAL%20Fixing%20 Broken%20Textbooks%20Report1.pdf.

2. Florida Virtual Campus, "2012 Florida Student Textbook Survey," 2012, www.open accesstextbooks.org/pdf/2012_Florida_Student_Textbook_Survey.pdf.

3. University of Florida, Office for Student Financial Affairs, "Cost of Attendance," 2016, www.sfa.ufl.edu/cost/.

4. Florida Virtual Campus, "2012 Florida Student Textbook Survey."

5. Florida Department of Education, "Executive Summary of HB 7019 Education Access and Affordability," 2016, www.fldoe.org/core/fileparse.php/7513/urlt/7019–16.pdf.

6. Peter Suber, "A Very Brief Introduction to Open Access," http://legacy.earlham.edu/ ~peters/fos/brief.htm.

7. Creative Commons, "What Is OER?" last modified February 8, 2016, https://wiki .creativecommons.org/wiki/What_is_OER%3F.

8. Isabel Elaine Allen and Jeff Seaman, "Opening the Textbook: Educational Resources in US Higher Education, 2015–16," Babson Survey Research Group, www.onlinelearning survey.com/reports/openingthetextbook2016.pdf.

Bibliography

Allen, Isabel Elaine, and Jeff Seaman. "Opening the Textbook: Educational Resources in US Higher Education, 2015–16." Babson Survey Research Group, 2016. www.online learningsurvey.com/reports/openingthetextbook2016.pdf.

Creative Commons. "What Is OER?" Last modified February 8, 2016. https://wiki .creativecommons.org/wiki/What_is_OER%3F.

Florida Department of Education. "Executive Summary of HB 7019 Education Access and Affordability." 2016. www.fldoe.org/core/fileparse.php/7513/urlt/7019–16.pdf.

Florida Virtual Campus. "2012 Florida Student Textbook Survey." 2012. www.openaccess textbooks.org/pdf/2012_Florida_Student_Textbook_Survey.pdf.

Senack, Ethan. "Fixing the Broken Textbook Market: How Students Respond to High Textbook Costs and Demand Alternatives." U.S. PIRG Education Fund & the Student PIRGs. 2014. www.uspirg.org/sites/pirg/files/reports/NATIONAL%20Fixing%20 Broken%20Textbooks%20Report1.pdf.

Suber, Peter. "A Very Brief Introduction to Open Access." http://legacy.earlham.edu/~peters/ fos/brief.htm.

University of Florida, Office for Student Financial Affairs. "Cost of Attendance." 2016. www.sfa.ufl.edu/cost.

ABOUT THE CONTRIBUTORS

KRISTINE ALPI is director of the William R. Kenan Jr. Library of Veterinary Medicine and adjunct assistant professor of population health and pathobiology at North Carolina State University. A subject specialist member of the NCSU Libraries' Alt-Textbook Team, she works closely with faculty on all aspects of promoting learning through the production of scholarly works.

PENNY BEILE is associate director for research, education, and engagement at the University of Central Florida Libraries. A consultant with extensive experience in information literacy assessment, Beile has worked with the Educational Testing Service and Project SAILS to develop content and recommend cut scores for standardized assessments of information literacy. Her research interests include assessing student learning as it relates to information literacy instruction and the ongoing validation of information literacy as a construct.

MELISSA CLAPP is director of library research, education, and outreach services at Wofford College's Sandor Teszler Library in South Carolina. Formerly, she was the instruction and outreach coordinator at Library West at the University of Florida, where she worked for thirteen years. She has published work on information literacy, library management, and digital humanities.

JOSH CROMWELL is the institutional repository coordinator for the University of Southern Mississippi Libraries. In this role, he oversees the operations of the university's institutional repository, the Aquila Digital Community. Through the institutional repository, he provides support for journal publishing, electronic theses and dissertations, event and lecture archiving, and research data. He also offers training for faculty regarding author rights, open access and other scholarly communication initiatives. He manages the libraries' open textbook program, which launched in fall 2015.

WILLIAM CROSS is the director of copyright and digital scholarship at the North Carolina State University Libraries. Trained as a lawyer and librarian, Cross provides legal and policy guidance and lectures nationally on digital citizenship and open culture. He leads the NCSU Libraries' Alt-Textbook Team.

ALICE DAUGHERTY is collections assessment and analysis librarian at Louisiana State University Libraries, where she has focused her career on statistics of library and information services. She writes and presents widely on issues of library services and collections. Currently, she serves on the Editorial Advisory Board for Emerald's *Advances in Library Administration and Organization.*

AIMEE DeNOYELLES is an instructional designer at the University of Central Florida's Center for Distributed Learning, where she assists faculty members in the design and development of online courses. Her research interests include e-textbooks, online discussion strategies, and technology and gender. DeNoyelles has published in several journals, including *Computers & Education, Journal of Online Learning and Teaching, Journal of Applied Research in Higher Education*, and *Journal of Special Education Technology.*

STACEY EWING is associate chair of the Humanities and Social Sciences Library West at the University of Florida. Her research interests include academic library technologies for students and accessibility services and resources for academic library patrons.

SHARON E. FARB is UCLA's associate university librarian for collection management and scholarly communication. Farb provides campus, statewide, and national leadership on the role of the public research library in higher education, focusing on organizing and preserving knowledge for present and future generations of students, faculty, and researchers. She has presented and written on copyright, intellectual property, content licensing, privacy, and intellectual freedom.

EMILY FRANK is a research and instruction librarian at Louisiana State University Libraries. She is the liaison to the College of Engineering and oversees the libraries' e-textbooks initiatives. She received her MLIS degree from the University of Kentucky and an international master's degree in digital library learning from universities in Norway, Estonia, and Italy through a program funded by the European Union.

APRIL HINES is the journalism and mass communications librarian for the University of Florida's George A. Smathers Libraries. Her research areas include face-to-face facilitation processes, library marketing and outreach, and social media engagement. She has presented and published on such topics as academic librarians and personal branding, using ethnic newspapers to reach underserved communities, and developing a library student ambassador program.

MICHAEL HUGHES is the collection development librarian for New York University Shanghai, as well as the reference and public services librarian at the Institute of Fine Arts at New York University in New York.

JIM MARTIN is an associate librarian in the Research and Learning Department at the University of Arizona Libraries, where he serves as a liaison librarian for physical sciences and mathematics. His research has focused on issues related to information resources management and needs assessment.

SARAH NORRIS is scholarly communication librarian at the University of Central Florida Libraries. In this role, she leads the UCF Libraries' scholarly communication and open access efforts, with an emphasis on scholarly publishing and copyright training and education. Her research interests include digital humanities and copyright implications in the digital environment, as well as open access efforts including the expanded use of OERs in the classroom.

JOHN RAIBLE is an instructional designer at the University of Central Florida's Center for Distributed Learning. In this role, he works with faculty to transition courses from face-to-face to the blended or online environment. His research areas include the integration of technology into online curriculums, accessibility for online learners, and the use of OER materials. He has presented at local, state, national, and international conferences, in addition to being published in multiple journals.

GREG RASCHKE is the associate director for collections and scholarly communication at the North Carolina State University Libraries. Among his administrative duties, Raschke leads partnerships in developing sustainable channels for scholarly communication and enhancing digitally enabled research and scholarship. He also leads efforts to support faculty and graduate students with emerging tools, programs, and services across the research life cycle.

COLLEEN SEALE, university librarian, serves as the collection manager for humanities and social sciences reference and as the selector and library liaison for women's and gender studies at the University of Florida's George A. Smathers Libraries. She has worked at the University of Florida for over twenty-five years and has published on several topics related to the academic library environment.

DAWN SETZLER is the UCLA Library's director of communications. As a senior communications officer with extensive experience in the nonprofit arena, Setzler plans, implements, and manages a broad range of communications activities, including public engagement and government relations, in support of the UCLA Library's strategic goals, mission, and objectives.

ELIZABETH SILER is the collection development librarian for the J. Murrey Atkins Library at the University of North Carolina Charlotte. She is keenly interested in textbook affordability, which has led her to start the Atkins Library E-Textbook Program; serve as the team leader of the Course Use Research Team for the Andrew W. Mellon Foundation-funded Charlotte Initiative: eBooks and the Academic Library Market; and work on a statewide task force focusing on textbook affordability for the University of North Carolina state system.

MADISON SULLIVAN is a libraries fellow at the North Carolina State University Libraries. Sullivan is a librarian for research and information services and external relations. She contributes to the NCSU Libraries' Alt-Textbook Project as a team member and faculty liaison.

NIAMH WALLACE is an assistant librarian in the Research and Learning Department at the University of Arizona Libraries. She is interested in issues of textbook affordability and serves as a social sciences liaison librarian.

INDEX

interface, of Faculty Textbook Database, 29–31
Internet access, at NYU Shanghai, 62

J
Journal of Chemical Education, 82

L
Learning Enhancement Center (LEC), 94, 98
librarians
Alt-Textbook project collaboration, 83–84
on Alt-Textbook project team, 76–77
DDA model and, 46–47
open textbooks, demonstration of value of, 100
training of faculty in Open Textbook Initiative, 97–98
UCF textbook affordability working group, 114–116
UCF working group, catalysts for, 105–107
UCF working group, nature of collaborative efforts, 107–113
UF, leveraging library materials/OERs, 124–128
library
Alt-Textbook project opens doors to, 83–84
cost of Atkins Library E-Textbook program to, 34–35
expenditures, decrease in, 25
lack of mentions on course syllabi, 122, 124–125
leadership in e-textbook availability for students, 13–14
open textbooks, reasons for, 92–93
textbook problem, efforts to address, 70–71
Library Bill of Rights (American Library Association), 60
library stories, 84
Library Tools Tab, 16–17
licensing
of alt-texts, 79
NYU Shanghai's electronic course materials and, 63
open-licensed/copyright-free versions of course materials, 109–111
for UAL e-books, 19–20
log-in, 48

Louisiana State University (LSU) Libraries
conclusion about, 53
DDA model, limitations of, 46–48
DDA model, shift away from, 48–49
e-book collection development, 45–46
e-textbook impact, 49–53

M
macro approach, 107
macro efforts, 108–109
Makerspace, 85
marketing
of Alt-Textbook project, 77–78, 83–84
of Atkins Library E-Textbook program, 36–38
faculty outreach for Atkins Library E-Textbook program, 31–33
of UF Library resources/OERs, 127–128
user experience of Atkins Library E-Textbook program marketing, 36–38
Martin, Jim, 13–22
micro approach, 107–108
micro efforts, 109–114
Modify tier, of Open Textbook Initiative, 95–96, 97
Moore, Kate, 48
MyiLibrary, 20

N
National Association of College Stores, 14
National Louis University, vii–x
NCSU Bookstores, 70
Nebraska Book Company, 51
New York University Abu Dhabi, 59
New York University Shanghai
conclusion about, 64–65
electronic course materials, 62–64
library collection development, 58–59
opening of, 57
print course materials, 59–62
textbooks, procurement of, 57–58
Norris, Sarah, 103–116
North Carolina State University Foundation, 72–73
"The North Carolina State University Libraries' Alt-Textbook Project" (Alpi, Cross, Raschke, & Sullivan), 69–86